Poverty and Christianity

Michael Taylor

Poverty and Christianity

Reflections at the Interface
between Faith and Experience

The Bernard Gilpin Pastoral Theology Lectures for 2000
University of Durham

scm press

0 334 02814 0

This edition first published 2000 by
SCM Press,
9–17 St Albans Place London N1 0NX

SCM Press is a division of
SCM-Canterbury Press Ltd

Typeset at Regent Typesetting, London
Printed in Great Britain by
Biddles Ltd, Guildford and King's Lynn

CONTENTS

to Adèle
with much love
'forty years on'

ACKNOWLEDGMENTS

I am grateful for the invitation to give the Bernard Gilpin Pastoral Theology Lectures for 2000 in the University of Durham and to those who listened to them patiently and discussed them with me at Ushaw College. Parts of this material, especially chapter 3, were presented to the Modern Churchpeople's Union Conference in 1999 and chapter 2 formed the substance of the J. C. Jones Memorial Lecture for 2000 in Wales under the auspices of the Church Missionary Society.

My thanks are also due to Maggie Clay for a great deal of cheerful and efficient practical help.

INTRODUCTION

Several colleagues and friends of mine visited Rwanda after the genocide in 1994. Some were there within days when the immediate aftermath of the slaughter was everywhere to see. Some were there within months and saw churches where hundreds of terrified people seeking sanctuary had been butchered, and mass graves that still heaved and cracked open with their dead. Not surprisingly, they came home traumatized.

I spent twelve memorable years of my life, as Director of Christian Aid, face-to-face with world poverty. I too went to Rwanda and many other places in Africa, Asia, Central and South America, Europe and the Pacific. I was often saddened and upset by what I saw, though just as often inspired by the resilience and courage of the people I met. I was never psychologically traumatized. I was, however, traumatized theologically. It was not my emotions but my Christian faith which often refused to function.

Rwanda was not, as it happened, the most striking example but it will serve to illustrate the point.

On a November afternoon in 1994 I found myself on a United Nations plane flying over the country and about to land at Goma, a small town in Zaire just over the border with Rwanda. The plane was small enough for me to see out of the front, directly ahead. What I saw I shall always think of as 'blue remembered hills'.

The town was surrounded by refugee camps, 'home' to almost a million Rwandans (not the only ones) who had fled literally for their lives from a murderous campaign to eliminate them, a campaign which, as the world now knows, reached genocidal proportions. The camps were also 'home' to many of the killers fearful of being killed in turn. The hills were turned blue by a myriad blue plastic sheets issued by the United Nations as shelter from sun and drenching rain.

I spent several days in and out of the camps. I walked on ground made up of volcanic ash. When dry the hardened lumps could cut into your feet. When wet it all turned into a sea of mud. I saw tree trunks moving horizontally, as if by magic, along the tops of the tall grasses, only to find they were carried by children from what little of the surrounding forest remained to provide fuel for cooking and to make shelters and pews! I sat on one of the pews when I went to church on Sunday in the open air.

I met a young mother in the camps with the same name as my own mother, carrying her child at her dry breasts. She asked for a blue plastic sheet. She said she was alone and had no one and nothing to protect her. I watched the distribution of food and noted the inevitable reliance on community 'leaders' who were as much feared as trusted. Some of the food fed the militia. Some of it was sold on. Some people were re-establishing small business enterprises within the camps. The vast majority, robbed of their land, had lost every vestige of an independent livelihood.

I did not see, as friends and colleagues did, the full horror of the original flight from Rwanda. I did not see the little town of Goma overwhelmed. I was not forced to get through by driving over the bodies of the dead. I was not traumatized like others were.

It was not my only experience of the cruel effects of war. I had seen them in Cambodia with its killing fields, in the Sudan, in Salvador, in Haiti and elsewhere. But what I saw in Rwanda were, for me, the worst.

During my visit I sat and listened to groups of pastors in the refugee camps and later, in Kigali, the capital of Rwanda, to the leaders of the churches who had stayed and not fled either to the camps or to Nairobi. They talked about what had happened and what should happen next. A good deal was said about 'truth'. The truth had to be told. It had to come out. Understandably, as in all such situations, a good deal of this talk had to do with the endless cycle of charge and countercharge, one group against another, Hutu and Tutsi; and 'truth' was a one-sided version of events in which the speaker was the innocent party and others were to blame. There was also talk of 'repentance'. People had to acknowledge what had happened, face up to their own part in it, accept that it was evil and start behaving differently. And then, encouraged by members of the ecumenical family from outside of Africa, there was much talk of 'reconciliation'. Rwandans who had once lived together, however uneasily, had to learn to live together again, forgiving and respecting each other and creating bonds of friendship and co-operation.

'Truth' and 'reconciliation' were already becoming good, strong words for me within the very different context of South Africa, but here they struck a false note and I found my inner-self largely at odds with those who were using them, since underlying them was the assumption that it was the wilful perversity of the Rwandan people which had created this tragedy and that it would be an equally 'will-full' volte-face on their part which would put it right. Sheer perversity lay at the root of the problem.

It was obvious to even the most inexperienced observer, however, that these people, leaders and led, killers and killed, despite the evil they had perpetrated, were victims far more than they were vicious. This is not the place, and I am not the person, to tell the long story of the Rwandan crisis,[1] but it includes many players and many factors beyond the control of those immediately involved: other countries in Africa, European colonial powers, cultural traditions of solidarity and authoritarianism reinforced if thought fit by colonial administrators, previous unrest, mistrust between more and less favoured groups, propaganda, and the endless and perhaps crucial struggle over scarce resources in one of the few countries in Africa which can reasonably be described as 'over-populated'.

So when I heard a good deal of talk, and easy talk by some, of repentance and reconciliation it seemed unhelpful and unreal mainly because it would need fundamental changes in the circumstances of these people before peace and reconciliation became a possibility, but also because it was hard to believe they would heap such un-numbered horrors on each other for no 'good' reason at all. But that is what the talk of 'repentance' fundamentally assumed. That assumption is prevalent in a great deal of Christian teaching and preaching that I have encountered in Christian attitudes to the poor and to the victims of war, not to mention many in Western congregations who are neither. It provides the background to theories of atonement and to frequent offers of divine forgiveness. The roots of 'sin' and of tragedies like the genocide in Rwanda lie in the end, it is assumed, in a kind of wilful or gratuitous disobedience or perversity which refuses to co-operate with God simply because it chooses not to, engaging instead in a mindless rebellion just for the sake of it. We choose to behave extremely badly and we can 'repent' of it and choose to behave otherwise.

Christian teaching about sin and evil are, needless to say, rather more sophisticated than that and to some of that sophistication we shall return. Enough has been said for the time being, however, to illustrate what I mean by 'theological trauma' when my own in-built Christian faith, inadequate and naïve maybe but still mine, and, even more so in this particular case, the Christianity being put to work by the churches on the bloody ground of Rwanda, refused to function. As a result I had to stop and think and it was not entirely like the cool, calm procedure, devoid of emotion that it may come to sound. The first two reflections which follow arose from similar though, for me, far more unsettling experiences of theological trauma. The first, on the 'normality' of suffering, was triggered off by my experience of famine in Africa and the second, on Christianity's lack of redemptive impact, by disastrous floods in Bangladesh.

The experience behind the other two reflections: on the

contribution of Christian faith to development policy in chapter 3 and on more productive ways of going about the struggle against oppressive poverty in chapter 4, was of a very different kind. Until I joined Christian Aid theology had been central to my life. I became interested in it as a teenager. I studied it at university. As a local Baptist minister I thought it my duty to teach it and preach it to others and get them to understand its importance. Later on, as a staff member of a theological college and member of a university theological faculty, I continued to teach it as well as struggle to make better sense of it for myself and others, and often engage in heated debates between various schools of thought. Though a generalist, theology was in a sense my profession and my world tended to revolve around it. Outed from the closet in 1985, it was discomforting to realize that many, many people, busily engaged in work which I regarded as close to the heart of what the gospel was all about, hardly engaged in theology at all or felt the need to do so. I had been much preoccupied with getting on with it. They found it easy to get on well enough without it. What for me was central was for them peripheral.

Several reactions, from defensiveness to capitulation, are likely to flow from such an experience, and they did; but among them should be, and I hope in my case it was, a renewed attempt to demonstrate the value of theology not just in its own world but in the world of politics and economics, government and civil society in which Christian Aid and similar agencies had to operate, and how it could undergird, nourish and enlighten the tasks in hand. The third and fourth chapters in this book reflect something of that attempt in writing,[2] but the proof or otherwise of its success lies, of course, in the active commitment in which theology did or did not play a constructive part.

All of the reflections which follow, including the brief concluding one on Christian hope, are exercises in what might be called 'pastoral cycling'. The pastoral cycle is by now well known to many of us. At its simplest it is an endless cycle of interactions between our faith and our life and work; between what we believe, what we experience and what we decide to do. Faith colours life and affects our work. Life and work bring with them new experiences which affect our faith. For much of the time these interactions are unselfconscious. For some of the time they are not. For various reasons we are stopped in our tracks and have to think again. One reason is that our experience, in my case of war and famine and flood, presents us with a very real challenge to our faith. Another reason is that we are not sure what to do, in my case in the face of world poverty. Where does our obedience as Christians lie? What action should we take? What policies should we adopt? How do we set about our task and how can we draw on our faith amongst other things to guide us? Pastoral cycling between faith and experience inevitably involves travelling round again where many, including ourselves, have travelled before. We cover old ground in the hope of appropriating it afresh: of 'seeing the place for the first time'. But pastoral cycling is also a never-ending journey forwards, since there are always new experiences to be had and more resources of Christian faith to discover. That is a particularly sensitive point for me. Poverty, though global, is still largely the burden of the South and the East; and the Christian church which a hundred years ago was the church of the West and the North is also now largely of the South and the East; but we still know far more about the faith and experience of the world's relatively well-off than of the world's poor or the faith of the church to which we all now belong. My own reading of Southern theology, let alone anything else, remains far too cursory. There is still a lot of learning to be done.

If any conclusion does emerge from these reflections and their underlying unease about the adequacy of Christian faith it is probably this: the validity of our theological work, whether systematic or practical, must be tested in many ways but no test is more important than whether or not it contributes to historical change in favour of the poorest. What for me is the bias of the gospel has to be the bias of theology.

1

THE NORMALITY OF SUFFERING

1. The famine

I could begin almost anywhere, as we shall see, but I will begin with the great famine in the Horn of Africa in 1984 and the massive relief efforts spearheaded by Bob Geldof, Live Aid and Band Aid which brought to prominence aid and development work as probably never before.

I did not myself visit the Horn of Africa until 1987. In the town of Mkele in Tigré, sandwiched between Ethiopia and Eritrea, still at war with each other at the time, I was shown the sites of camps to which thousands of desperately hungry men, women and children had fled. They left behind their plots of dry land, thirsty for rain, where no crops would grow. They came looking for food and found instead the diseases from which thousands of them died.

On the same day we walked up a gentle slope beyond the little town to see what was being done to prevent the recurrence of such a disaster. We could not go far on grounds of security, but far enough to witness a sight almost 'biblical' in its proportions. As many as two thousand women were making the earth move: digging it out with their hands and a few spades, carrying it on sacks between them or in the half-a-dozen old wheelbarrows at their command, dumping it along a seemingly endless line crossing the landscape, trampling and damping it down to form a dam twelve metres high.

The women were preparing to 'harvest' the water: 500,000 cubic metres of it! When the rains did come, instead of running off the land and taking yet more topsoil with it, they would collect it in the vast reservoir they were creating and then control its flow out to the land on the other side of the dam where it would sink gently in and nourish the ground.

By contrast I was introduced to a farmer and his wife and nine children who had decided to stay at home even when the drought was at its worst. With hindsight they were probably wise to do so, avoiding the disease-ridden camps and on hand to take advantage of the rain should it come. But the cost of doing so was all too evident. The family had two 'houses'. One looked derelict, built of sun-dried bricks but shorn of its metal window frames and corrugated iron roof, open to the heat of the sky. The other was round, running up to a pointed roof, crude and fragile and made entirely of grasses. The brick house had been the fruit of relative but short-lived economic success. A small surplus had enabled it to be built. The surplus had now turned rapidly into a deficit. The persistent farmer had sown his crop but without the rains it had failed. He had then sown a second crop. This time it was blighted by pest. He had sold the metal frames and the roof of his home to buy food for his family and seeds for a third sowing only to meet with failure yet again. He said it was important 'not to give up but keep on trying'.

Fifteen years after 1984, in 1999 and January 2000, there were reports, often lost in the news of wars and rumours of wars in Africa, Asia and Europe, of famine in the Horn of Africa, and drought, and of war between Ethiopia and Eritrea as serious as before. Some said even more so – but that is another story to which we must return (in chapter 2).

This African famine raised a host of important issues. It challenged, for example, easy talk of 'natural disasters' due in this instance to lack of rain. The causes were not in fact natural or mysterious or beyond human control. They could be traced to an onslaught on the environment and not just in the Horn of Africa, to deforestation and soil erosion during the twentieth century. It also challenged what was meant by a 'famine'. People died from disease as much as from hunger. In other 'famines' they die from war. Food was never in short supply. The world, even probably Africa, had more than enough and to spare. It was the distribution of food that failed, coupled with the fact that hungry people had no money to buy it, in sharp contrast to the better off who, in the West, may grow nothing and have no land or skills to do so, but nevertheless shop and eat their fill.

The 1984 famine also illustrated that whilst a vast flow of emergency relief aid, funded by governments and charitable donations, may be inevitable once a disaster has occurred, it is fundamentally flawed as a way of dealing with the underlying problem. First, it diminishes and demeans people who would much rather look after themselves and earn their own living, and are as capable of doing so as anybody else. Aid perpetuates their dependence on the goodwill of others, or the lack of it. Second, it obscures the fact that over much the same period of time in the mid-1980s, the Horn of Africa lost billions of pounds worth of potential income due to a fall in commodity prices, including the price of coffee, on world markets. This loss was far in excess of the three to five billion which the Horn of Africa received in aid. A more equitable trading system would have enabled Ethiopia and Tigré to feed their own people and enjoy a measure of dignity.

But what struck me most forcibly when I visited the sites of the death camps and saw the epic struggle of two thousand women and heard the story of a single farmer, an equally epic struggle in its own small way, was the scale of suffering they all represented. It was well beyond anything I had encountered or even considered before. On reflection I came to think of it as the pervasiveness of suffering but finally came to describe it as its 'normality'. It rapidly turned itself into a challenge to my Christian faith.

My faith, like that of most others, had long had to come to

terms with suffering. Within my family circle, like any other, we knew of illness, bad genes, bereavement, accidents, failure and misfortune. We have a handicapped daughter. Early on in my professional life, as a pastor, I probably had more than the average number of encounters with human pain and sorrow. The same could be said of doctors, nurses, paramedics, the police, social workers and all those confidants who listen quietly in the most unexpected corners of life. And like others I had been aware that in many parts of the world there were people far worse off than myself. All of this, however, had been bearable and excusable when perceived as the exception rather than the rule. Suffering was like the clouds which occasionally darkened an otherwise clear and often sunny sky beneath which it was appropriate to chant: the earth is the Lord's and the fullness thereof.

But on that visit to Ethiopia and Tigré in 1987 it struck home to me as it had not done before that human suffering was not an aberration but the norm. The camps of disease and death came to symbolize the seriousness and depth of it; the women toiling in their thousands came to symbolize the extent of it; and the farmer repeatedly tackling failure by sowing his seeds over and over again, the persistence of it. Looking back over history most human lives for most of their brief span, it now seemed to me, had been miserable and unfulfilled. Looking out over the globe billions remain in abject poverty and three-quarters of the world's people remain markedly worse off than the remaining quarter. I, like others, had often thought that there was too much suffering and that much of it was arbitrary and unjust. Now it occurred to me that most people had suffered for most of the time.

This 'normality' may not, on reflection, be as bad as at first it seems. Whilst the statistics of poverty, whether we are talking in historical or contemporary terms, can hardly be challenged, my negative view of what I have loosely called 'suffering' is largely from the outside. Is it seen as quite so negative from the inside?

Even the visit to Ethiopia and Tigré in 1987 had its cheerful aspects. Poor communities are places of hospitality and culture. Children play. People dance and celebrate. They worship and observe their rites of passage. Their faith is strong. Their spirits are often high, higher than those of their visitors who deplore their misfortunes. The sophisticated affluence of Western culture is not really known to them and therefore hardly missed. A simpler way of living, in stronger and more stable communities, may even be gain rather than loss. What you are born into and have always been used to is in any case easier to deal with than what you reluctantly have to adjust down to or fear you might. The very nature of normality is that it is not particularly notice-able, so that what from the outside look like dire conditions are from the inside simply everyday realities which do not preclude pleasure or satisfaction.

This more sanguine, not to say romantic, view of the suffering which is everywhere does not fit easily, however, with the apparently universal wish to be free of it and to climb out of poverty towards a better standard of living, education and healthcare, and a greater degree of self-determination. If poverty really is not half as bad as it looks, without denying the cultural, spiritual and moral riches of its inhabitants, it is for those who live in poverty to say so. In general they don't.

The 'normality' of suffering remained, therefore, as an experi-enced challenge to my Christian faith. I suppose I had previously assumed that, given it was exceptional, suffering was also excus-able and explicable. Christianity could cope with it. In a fragile world, for example, accidents could and did happen. Punishment had its place. We did wrong and thoughtless things or took foolish decisions and suffered the consequences. And hard times could be good for us and tough challenges could get the best out of us. All these almost common-sense themes, not surprisingly, found their way into Christian teaching. My Christianity had coped with suffering. But this sudden and sobering awareness of it as 'normal' made the issue far more pressing, as personal tragedy often does for others, and made me wonder how Christianity could cope with it all or possibly defend it.

'Theodicy' is the long tradition of hard thinking by which Christianity has mounted its defence, trying as it does to reconcile our faith in a powerful and loving God with such appalling realities as the famine of 1984. Whilst most of its arguments contain more than a grain of truth, no one I suspect would ever claim that any of them are entirely satisfactory. That would be to deny an indisputable fact. We are, as human beings, surrounded by mystery. What we know is considerable, but what we don't know is immeasurable. The extent of our unknowing is suggested to the imagination by the physical scale of the universe where our small planet is virtually lost in the limitless reaches of space, containing galaxy after galaxy, universe beyond universe, and black holes which seem to incarnate eternity in time; and where every short walk we take along the surface of the earth, thinking our thoughts and wondering about ourselves, is an almost mystical experience, balancing on the edge of the unfathomable. We do not know and cannot finally and satisfactorily answer our own questions when we try to make sense of the mystery of how and why we are here and what exactly we understand by 'here' in any case.

The point is, however, that faced with the 'normality' of suffering the answers to the problem of evil which will always be somewhat unsatisfactory become even more so.[1] Take the two which are most familiar. The first puts the evil in the world down mainly to our own perverse behaviour. It is our fault. There are reasonable ways of behaving, with sensible constraints which will lead to the wellbeing of everyone. We choose to ignore them and we suffer the consequences. The causes of poverty in the world are clear evidence of that, as were the causes of the famine in 1984. It was partly the result of our failure to be good stewards of creation. Given a garden created by God for us to water and till, we had over-exploited its resources to the extent of robbing it of all its trees, and as the trees disappeared so did the topsoil, and with the trees and the soil went the balanced conditions which had previously allowed the gentler rains to nourish the ground and the ground to yield its crops. The famine was also aggravated by war. More fundamentally, it was the direct result of a world economy which did not allow the Ethiopians to earn their livelihood by getting a fair price for the few commodities like coffee they had to sell. The famine was essentially the result of a failure of stewardship and a lack of justice; and what was true in that one instance has been equally true in many others. So we have only ourselves to blame.

This iron chain of cause and effect can be defended. It provides us with a reliable or predictable world to live in and with what has been called a 'moral universe' where bad deeds will have bad results and good deeds, fortunately, will lead to good results. The familiar objections and difficulties, however, only seem to be intensified by the scale of the poverty and misery that confronted me. The consequences of human misdemeanours, for example, seem even more out of proportion. If they are in any sense a 'punishment' or retribution, then the punishment no longer fits the crime. And worse, the repercussions seem to fall far more heavily on the relatively innocent: the hundreds of thousands in the famine of 1984 who died, let alone the unnumbered poor of history, than on the guilty: such as the more powerful minorities who eat well and always live to tell the tale, so that the original injustice is only compounded. It does not seem as though occasionally and unfortunately and unavoidably the innocent suffer, but always and everywhere. It is an 'immoral universe', not a moral one.

The second most familiar argument is that this extremely hazardous world is good for us. It is good for us in the sense we have just referred to. The disasters it confronts us with are part of an 'ordering', natural and moral, which we should be far worse off without. (There is, of course, an even more 'Machiavellian' and indefensible version of that argument: that we live in the best of all possible worlds where hidden hands and mechanisms, economic and moral, ensure that even the most rapacious economic acts result in the common good and competitive self-interest benefits everyone so that in the end 'losers' become 'winners'.) And the hazardous nature of existence is good for us because it presents us with the kind of challenges to intellectual, moral and spiritual growth without which we would never reach our full potential as competent and resourceful human beings. Again the old objection, that the cost of growing up seems to be too high, has only intensified. For Dostoievski the cost was vividly portrayed in the immense, but occasional cruelties of a despot: 'It's not worth the tears of that one tortured child.'[2] For me, in the context of the 1984 famine, it had become the near universal suffering of the humanity that was supposed to be raised by that suffering to its full stature.

In these and other ways what I have called the 'normality' of suffering made inevitably unsatisfactory 'theodicies' overwhelmingly so. It could be said that I was being swept towards this conclusion, with all its ability to challenge and undermine my Christian faith, on a tide of emotion. That does not necessarily make it invalid. Emotion, and the insights it may yield, are not to be despised. It is as well, however, to try to complement emotion with careful reflection. So I turned to three writers on theodicy, partly because they had proved helpful in the past but also because they have in their own ways faced up to this dimension of the problem of evil which some might call its 'enormity' but which I have called its overwhelming 'normality', a normality which struck me so forcibly as I confronted the aftermath of the Ethiopian famine of 1984.

2. *Evil and the God of Love*

John Hick's *Evil and the God of Love* was first published in 1966, since when it has inspired a whole corpus of writing on theodicy.[3] It takes a broadly Irenaean approach to the problem of evil without denying the valid insights of the Augustinian. We compound evil and bring much calamity on ourselves, but basically suffering is not punishment but the necessary condition of our growing up to be the children of God:

> God has ordained a world which contains evil – real evil – as a means to the creation of the infinite good of a Kingdom of Heaven within which His creatures will have come as perfected persons to love and serve him, through a process in which their own free insight and response have been an essential element.[4]

'A world which contains evil' is a means to an end. It functions as a sort of moral and spiritual 'outward-bound course' (my words, not Hick's) providing the challenges without which our characters would not develop and our human potential would not be discovered or realized. It is also a world where God's good presence is sufficiently veiled and ambiguous to allow us to respond and relate to him freely rather than being overawed and compelled to do so. The corollary is that in our uncertainty about his ultimate benevolence and whether we are secure within it we are free to react far more negatively and destructively than if our safety was beyond doubt.

In a long, clear and detailed argument covering many issues Hick confronts head-on the objection that suffering and evil are excessive and unjustly distributed. He even refers to 'famine':

> Let the hypothesis of a divine purpose of soul-making be adopted, and let it be further granted that an environment which is to serve this purpose cannot be a permanent hedonistic paradise but must offer to man real tasks, challenges, and problems. Still the question must be asked: Need the world contain the more extreme and crushing evils which it in fact contains? Are not life's challenges often so severe as to be self-defeating when considered as soul-making influences? Man must (let us suppose) cultivate the soil so as to win his bread by the sweat of his brow; but need there be gigantic famines . . . from which millions have so miserably perished? . . . when

such things happen we can see no gain to the soul, whether of the victim or of others, but on the contrary only a ruthlessly destructive process which is utterly inimical to human values ... It is true that sometimes ... there are sown and there come to flower even in the direst calamity graces of character that seem to make even that calamity itself worthwhile ... But it may also fail to happen, and instead of gain there may be sheer loss ... affliction may crush the character and wrest from it whatever virtues it possessed.[5]

Hick makes three points by way of reply. First, evil is excessive (compare my word 'normality') only in relation to other evils. Once famines like that of 1984 are removed from the reckoning, then lesser 'routine' evils like the lack of rainfall in a particular locality and the subsequent failure of the farmer's crop become excessive in their turn; and there is no stopping the logic of the argument until any evil or testing experience is regarded as excessive. Second, with regard to the totally meaningless, uneven, irrational distribution of evil, if it were seen to be entirely reasonable and justified and an instrument for good it would evoke no passion or generous help. In 1984 Bob Geldof would not have been inspired to create Live Aid and Band Aid and five billion pounds would not have been raised for famine relief (not that any of that money reflected unambiguously the better, more disinterested spirit of Western man rediscovered in the face of disaster). The rationale of excessive suffering is mysterious, not obvious, and must remain so as part of a world in which true goodness can occur.

Third, Hick reflects on the sheer destructiveness of this excessive evil. It might be justified if it succeeded in bringing men and women to their full stature. It can never be justified if it simply crushes their spirit, and worse, reduces them to even greater perversity. The evidence here, as Hick admits, is not reassuring. For him, however, the final test is an eschatological one. It comes at the 'end' of the affair but not now. The process must be judged by the final outcome. Logically it is possible that it will fail. 'Morally', however, it seems 'impossible that the infinite resourcefulness of infinite love working in unlimited time should be eternally frustrated, and the creature reject its own good, presented to it in an endless range of ways'.[6]

But in this scenario of a continuing, infinitely drawn-out but ultimately successful process lies, for me, the problem (though as we have said no one can expect a theodicy without a problem since we cannot have a world without mystery: we don't know far more than we do). In *Evil and the God of Love* and elsewhere[7] Hick suggests that if soul-making were not as it were successfully completed in this life (or in this outward-bound school) it will be completed in another or in one or more of a succession of lives or incarnations (like serial purgatories) throughout 'unlimited time'. Presumably, however, if the problem is not to recur ad infinitum, God will have to use what Hick describes as God's 'infinite resourcefulness' to devise an environment which preserves God's necessary distance from us, so allowing us to respond to love in freedom, but is more adept than this one at wooing us and winning us. Persistence will not be sufficient to avoid infinite frustration and ensure success. If it is accepted that the world as it is is largely unsuccessful at soul-making, it follows that an endless succession of similar worlds is likely to be equally unsuccessful. God will therefore need to change tactics and, if so, why not sooner rather than later?

3. *Face to Face*

To turn to a second writer, Frances Young calls her book: *Face to Face*, a 'narrative essay'.[8] It tells the story of Arthur, her eldest child, and her responses as a mother, a Christian, a professional theologian and an ordained minister, to his profound disabilities. My own daughter is mentally handicapped but, as far as one can tell, the burden of it, though heavy at times, has been lighter than the burden of Arthur's disability. Young is well able to appreciate the many positive aspects to her family's relationships with Arthur including the games, the laughter, the achievements and the fun. For me, however, his disability, which even after long and painful treatment made him scarcely able to walk and even now leaves him unable to make more than a few, hard to recognize, sounds, and still incontinent, is of a similar order of magnitude to the suffering represented by the great famine of 1984. It was not 'exceptional' or 'abnormal'. It was not an extremely unfortunate part of life but not the whole. It struck me as excessive and overwhelming. Arthur in a microcosmic way, like hunger and poverty in a macrocosmic way, seemed to represent the 'normality' of human sorrow and suffering. Young, through sheer force of circumstance if for no other reason, has had to face up to the enormity or 'normality' of evil. I was therefore once again especially interested in what she had to say.

Young notes, almost in passing, the familiar theodicies which regard suffering as the consequence of sin or as necessary if we are to mature as God's children. They make valid points and echo her experience but they are not particularly satisfying given the extreme case of Arthur.[9] For Young a more satisfying response to Arthur's disability at the level of theological reflection, barely indistinguishable here from a lived-out spirituality, seems to lie in a further example of the paradoxical theology to which she is drawn and from which she believes we cannot escape. In this instance it refers to both the presence and the absence of God.

The absence of God has partly to do with the mystery and unknowability of God, once again quite rightly affirmed. It also speaks of God's necessary withdrawal in order to grant us the freedom to respond in love because we choose to and not because we must. If God is too blatantly obvious in all his goodness, justice and love then we are simply overwhelmed. This familiar point in theodicy, also made by Hick, is given fresh colour and intensity, though probably not a very different meaning, by reference to Simone Weil. She speaks of Creation as a voluntary abandonment or abdication. It is a renunciation and sacrifice:

God already voids himself of his divinity by the Creation . . . His love maintains in existence, in a free and autonomous existence, beings other than himself, beings other than the good . . . Through love he abandons them to affliction and sin. For if he did not abandon them they would not exist. His presence would annul their existence as a flame kills a butterfly . . . The evil which we see everywhere in the world in the form of affliction and crime is a sign of the distance between us and God. But this distance is love . . .[10]

God's absence, permitting sin and the demonic, is what allows our independent existence. It carries, however, dark ramifications and in the passion of Christ we see God bearing the painful consequences of his own act of creative love, taking responsibility for all the 'goneawayness', not ignoring what has occurred but entering into it to heal and reintegrate or make 'at-one'.[11]

For Young, therefore, the 'answer' or 'solution' to the problem of suffering is Job's answer: a sense of the presence of God. No argument can prove it: 'Yet to the discerning eye of faith . . . the man with arms outstretched on the cross can become a clue to the presence of God in the midst of all the world's tragedy. A God who takes responsibility for the awful mess that his creation has got into . . .' In his presence our protests and doubts, like Job's, are silenced. 'Face to face with God,' says Young, 'the problems do not disappear but they do appear different.'[12]

Whilst hesitating to respond to such an experienced, spiritual and poetic (Young includes poetry in her writings) 'theodicy' with prosaic arguments, inevitably questions arise. I have two. First, is God's 'abandonment' of us as wise or as necessary as it is made out to be? The obvious analogy is that of a human relationship between parent and child. The children need freedom to be themselves and make their own decisions with their consequent achievements and mistakes. Wise parents will therefore withdraw and give children the 'space' they require. But children, like adults, cannot have complete independence nor would it represent the best for them. We are dependent as well as independent. We are what we are because of our interdependence with others as much as because of our freedom and autonomy. Is there not something like a 'happy medium', as against the extremes of an overbearing presence on the one hand and abandonment on the other, whereby wise parents leave their children to be themselves and make their own way and yet remain as a guiding and preventing presence giving unfailing if unobtrusive support? To recognize how often such a presence can seem like interference and become unproductive is not to deny the positive role it can and frequently does play and, if it is within the wit of man to approximate to it, is it not within the power and wisdom of God? 'Abandonment' as Young, following Simone Weil, describes it, appears to be excessive.

But if the notion of 'abandonment' is problematic, so is that of the presence of God which silences doubt. For one thing, it would seem to offer us a 'knowingness' about God which God's absence, not to say abandonment of us, is designed to rule out. There is a world of difference between being left to live without God and being left with a kind of pretence: knowing God is 'really' there whilst appearing not to be. (Compare the comment in *The Independent* for 19 October 1999 that if the Chancellor is known to tax by stealth then it is no longer by stealth.) If God is known to obscure his presence deliberately in order not to overwhelm us, then his presence is not that obscure. If we are that 'knowing' about his absence, then his strategy is undermined. Or again, presumably when God's presence is made abundantly clear to Job and, through the cross, to Frances Young, clear enough that is to silence doubt, that awareness does not overwhelm them to the extent that their God-given freedom is thereafter denied them and they fall in love and trust God because they must and not because it is something they have chosen and wish to do. And if that is so now in God's appearances to Job and to believers in Christ, then why could God not have made that equally the case all along? If God's presence now can be productive of a free response in love, then why not then when God first created us?

It is almost as if Young is herself uneasy when she comments sympathetically on a paper by Ian Cohen in which he asks whether there is 'something defective in God which allowed him to be forgiven his failure to protect adequately and always be worthy of dependence'.[13] If so, of course, the problem for theodicy is not 'solved' but dissolved. The problem of reconciling evil with a good and all-powerful God is no longer a problem once God's power is compromised – a problem to which we shall return when we look at the third of our three writers.

4. *Love's Endeavour, Love's Expense*

W. H. Vanstone's book *Love's Endeavour, Love's Expense*,[14] arose, as far as I know, out of no overwhelming encounter with evil but from the working experience of a parish priest and the many encounters, with evil and with good, that that entails. It does, however, in a quite different way from Hick and Young, face up to what I have called the 'normality' of sorrow and suffering brought home to me by the Ethiopian famine of 1984. It does so by giving suffering and evil no positive value whatsoever, nor any necessary if highly problematic role to play. It is not primarily a necessary condition for soul-making. It is not the inevitable condition of our autonomy over against an otherwise overwhelming divine presence. It is indeed 'normality' itself. Basically, it is a feature of the uncreated raw material or 'chaos', 'without form or void' (Gen. 1.2) out of which in love God sets out to make a world. The order which love manages to establish out of chaos as it goes about its expensive task is the abnormal or exception to the otherwise general rule of mis-rule.

The picture is, of course, more complicated. The evil of chaos, as hostile and threatening as the Israelites found the sea and the great deep, is compounded in two ways. Both find echoes in more familiar theodicies and in the writings of Hick and Young.

First, human beings, who are made and called by God to be co-workers in reducing primal chaos to order and turning evil to good, fail to co-operate. The reasons once again have to do with the ambiguity of God's presence or God's absence which allows us, positively, the freedom to choose and be ourselves but, more negatively, allows us to misinterpret God's wisdom and love as indifference and, in our subsequent fear and insecurity, fall into self-regarding and destructive forms of behaviour.

Second, creating a world or indeed anything from a more just social order to a work of art has its risks and they are risks for a Creator God as well as for creative human beings. Vanstone refers to the precariousness of this activity:

> As the artist exceeds his known powers, his work is precariously poised between success and failure, between triumph and tragedy: it may be that the work of art is marred beyond redemption . . . [15]

By definition, to create is to venture into the unknown to a greater or lesser degree. For God it is to an absolute degree. Creative acts may carry with them the best and most loving of intentions. The outcome may well be as predicted and desired, but it can be unexpectedly negative, in which case the creative task becomes even more of a struggle than before. As a result, if the primary reality is creative activity, God with us turning 'chaos' to good order and making a home for us, there is a secondary reality. Corrective or redemptive activity is also necessary in order to win us back from destructive into constructive behaviour and to repair as it were the damage that arises when false moves are made in the creative process. It is conceivable that when God made man, both aspects of this secondary reality came very much to the fore. The result of giving man his freedom was infinitely more negative and damaging than God had imagined. God proceeds to bear the cost of it, an insight which recalls the similar insight of Simone Weil.

According to Vanstone, therefore, I do not have to justify or give any kind of reasonable account of monstrous evil or the 'normality' of suffering. Its status is precisely the evil void which God with us will turn to good.

This, for me, is a richly satisfying theodicy, but there hovers about it the suspicion that it attempts to resolve the problem by dissolving it. God may be entirely good and loving but not what we really understand by God. At the beginning 'he' does not appear to be in control. He is confronted by disordered and uncontrolled chaos. And as he embarks on creation he is not all-knowing or all-wise. He makes mistakes – some so disastrous they merely compound the problem he sets out to overcome.

Vanstone mounts a skilful argument in favour of God's 'godliness' despite the mistakes and once again, as with Hick, it is 'eschatological' in character. In Vanstone's theodicy, in contrast to Hick's, it is not so much that God will with hindsight turn out to be demonstrably loving; rather he will turn out to be demonstrably all-powerful. He will not only overcome the disastrous, unpredicted outcomes of his creative moves, he will so integrate, or we may say 'reconcile', them with his purposes that the end result will be enhanced.[16] The world God makes with us will then be a better world than if the false moves, and presumably everything that is painfully learnt from them, had never happened. God will ultimately master the chaos even if he has not, and apparently cannot, master it yet. We are still left, however, with a radically different understanding of God from that which traditional theodicies have assumed: God makes mistakes which God cannot avoid; God lacks foreknowledge of God's own actions; and God as well as the women and men God creates has to go through a process of learning as painful as, 'in the end', it is successful.

5. The end of theodicy

Faced in Ethiopia, as it were, with the 'normality' of suffering, my immediate reaction was to dismiss all the attempts I knew of to reconcile it with faith in a loving and powerful God as overwhelmingly unsatisfactory. Having paused to reflect a little more carefully, with the help of Christian thinkers who in their different ways address the issue not just of the existence of evil but of the enormity and ubiquity of evil, the sense of dissatisfaction remains (and no doubt they share it!). They offer a wealth of telling insights, born of experience, knowledge and argument, into the inevitable and enormous expense of fostering free human beings and making a home for them, but those insights stubbornly refuse to add up to a convincing whole. God's character can be defended, but not God's power: if he is good and 'godly' he is not 'godlike'. Reading Hick, one feels God is not sufficiently resourceful. Reading Young, one feels God has failed to counterbalance a necessary distance with a wise presence which 'prevents us everywhere'. Reading Vanstone, one feels that God has more to learn than is good for God's reputation. We come away from all three richer in our human understanding, not least of some of what might be called the 'dynamics of creativity', but without a satisfactory theodicy.

One option is to call a halt to the whole enterprise and announce 'the end of theodicy'. This could take either of two forms. The first is to stop believing in the God which theodicy tries to defend. That could mean a kind of intellectual acknowledgment that the failure of theodicy proves that such a God does not exist. Or it could mean making a moral judgment that even if God does exist he is morally indefensible and is not to be believed in or trusted. Or it could mean believing in a different kind of God, shorn of the trappings of omnipotence, persistent and unfailing in her love for us, but having to learn how to love effectively for our good. To believe in such a God could not, however, leave unchallenged or untouched other aspects of our

Christian believing, most obviously the hope that at the end of this massive learning curve 'all shall be well and all manner of thing shall be well'. If God is so vulnerable to the pitfalls which lie in the path of a lover, how can faith guarantee that love will eventually succeed?

The second way of announcing the end of theodicy is to accept that we don't know and cannot know the ultimate explanation for suffering and evil, especially where it is on such a scale that it looks more like the rule than the exception. This is not the same as saying, as some theodicies tend to say, that we don't know but we know why we don't know, and that is because if we did know God's claim on us would be so overwhelmingly obvious that we would have no choice but to submit to his friendly overtures. And it is not the same as saying that we don't know but if we did, or when we do, it would or will be fine. That is tantamount to saying almost airily that suffering and evil are a puzzling mystery but not really a problem. To say that we don't know is to eschew any attempt, for example in pastoral situations where those who suffer look for comfort, to justify or explain what has happened or to put people off with surface comments about more immediate causes which do little to address the underlying issue. To say we do not know is to say quite frankly that we do not know. There is no explanation and no excuse that we know of.

It is most unlikely, however, that most of us as Christian believers will opt for 'the end of theodicy' in either of these two ways. Instead we shall keep on trying, as in a sense this chapter has been trying, to reconcile our belief in a good and loving God with suffering and evil, however difficult a task it proves to be. In which case we might pause to ask 'Why?' If we reject 'the end of theodicy' in one sense we might ask about 'the end of theodicy' in another. What is its purpose, and for what 'end' shall we go on pursuing these tortuous and never-ending debates?

6. Theologies of the South

An admittedly cursory look at what might be called the 'theologies of the South', of Africa and Asia and South America, reveals what at first sight is a curious fact. They do not engage in theodicy very much, if at all. Rather than putting an end to the debate, they hardly begin it. This is curious, because theologies of the South might be thought of as the theologies of the poor to an extent that the theological traditions we have been considering, largely of the North and of the West, have never been of the poor. The theologies of the South were born in the rough cradle of ubiquitous suffering, poverty and injustice: deep, widespread and persistent. They know evil not as the exception but as the rule. They, above all, might have been expected to engage in 'theodicy' as a prime theological pursuit, if not to defend God then to challenge the God who allows the poor to suffer so much and for so long. But apparently they don't. We will look briefly at Africa, Asia and South America in turn.

In 1995 John Parratt in *Reinventing Christianity*,[17] attempted a survey of African theology today. Throughout its two hundred and twelve pages, theodicy is never mentioned except for one passing reference to suffering as possibly 'a means to a higher good'. This silence does not mean that suffering in the form of poverty and oppression is ignored. Far from it. It is central to one of what Parratt regards as the two main concerns of African theology. One is to relate Christianity to African culture, with its sense of solidarity, respect for human lives, and for community with the living and with the ancestors. It is a deeply religious culture. The other is to address contemporary political issues. The task of theology is essentially practical. It has to do with orthopraxis rather than orthodoxy: taking sides with God to overcome oppression and social disturbance and eradicate poverty. Liberation is a central theme of the Bible as it is of much African theology.

If we ask why theodicy is ignored, Parratt's survey offers us one or two clues. First, any attempt to reconcile suffering with the loving purposes of God is not on the agenda. Other issues are far more pressing and in any case the 'normality' of suffering, which shocked this one Westerner at least, is for the African so normal and so much part of everyday life that it is unremarkable. What matters is not to explain or justify it but to be rid of it and achieve wholeness of life in community. Second, theodicy may come under suspicion, in so far as it is recognized at all, as an example of the tendency of Western theology to over-intellectualize instead of concentrating on practical action.

But third, Western theology, including theodicy, comes under suspicion as the theology of the oppressor. It is Western and it is white. At best that would mean it has different interests and that its conceptual tools are inappropriate for black African Christians. More sinister is the possibility that it not only deals with white rather than black problems, but actually advances the oppressor's cause. This criticism was made very clearly in the Southern African *Kairos Document*[18] when it dismissed 'State Theology' as bowing too readily to the powers that be and 'Church Theology' as seeking reconciliation without justice. But it can also be made of the West's preoccupation with creeds and christologies and doctrines of atonement. Its concern or unconscious purpose is to maintain oppression. Intellectual debates change nothing, whereas the praxis of liberation does. Hence Manas Buthelezi, quoted by Parratt, is wary of a 'theology of tranquillity and dogmatic polish in times of restlessness due to people's alienation from the wholeness of contemporary life . . .'[19]

Applied to 'theodicy' which, as we have noted, the survey and therefore apparently African theology scarcely mentions, this raises the possibility that theodicy is too busy explaining and justifying human suffering rather than recognizing it for the evil that it is and bending the energies of theology to the task of getting rid of it. The 'end' or purpose of theodicy is to maintain the status quo rather than change it; and even if that is not its deliberate purpose it tends to have that effect, so cutting the nerve of action.

Turning to Asia and Sri Lanka, Aloysius Pieris, in *An Asian Theology of Liberation*, shares the same two concerns of African theology: 'inculturation' and 'liberation',[20] but here there is a much tighter interrelation between the two. The culture in question is again deeply religious and also pluralistic. It includes Islam, Hinduism and Buddhism. The task of Christianity is not to supersede the non-Christian religions, nor with Karl Barth on the one hand or Karl Marx on the other to be against religion as such as intrinsically ungodly or inhuman or both; but to ally itself with religion and draw on the potential of religion for achieving emancipation or 'liberation'. At one level this refers to the freedom from oppression or 'enforced poverty' which is the goal of African political theology and South American liberation theology. It means being involved with the God who is undoubtedly on the side of the poor and oppressed. But at another level 'emancipation' draws on the deeper resources of religion, Christian and non-Christian, to free us from attachment and dependence and from servitude not to human oppressors but to mammon and material possessions, preparing us for that true poverty which is chosen and life enhancing. Theology is: 'a Christian participation in and a christic explication of all that happens at the deepest zone of a concrete ethos where religiousness and poverty, each in its liberative dimension, coalesce to forge a common front against mammon'.[21] Religious movements are too easily institutionalized and filtered and become a means of enslavement, but at heart they are characteristically driven by a revolutionary impetus. Once again, any attempt to explain suffering and evil is set aside for the deeply religious task of bringing evil to an end.

A second Asian theologian, Eleazar Fernandez of the Philippines, does not set theodicy aside. He discusses it in *Toward a Theology of Struggle*.[22] He does not, however, practise it. There may be unresolved questions about undeserved suffering, but the main answer is clear: suffering for the most part is 'a product of history and a creation of people'.[23] Any attempt to obscure that fact is to be resisted. Fernandez accepts that 'suffering needs an explanation, whereby the sufferer can at least make sense of what he or she is undergoing'[24] and he reviews some of the explanations that have been offered. They contain echoes of the theodicies we have already discussed. Nature, for example, is not yet fully under control (compare the argument that the uncreated chaos has yet to be raised to order). Suffering is the cost of progress (compare the argument that the vale of soul-making is necessarily difficult and demanding and morally offensive). Again, we are estranged and alienated from our true being (compare the references to God's absence or abandonment and God's consequent attempts to reconcile). God also suffers, absorbing our historical suffering into his eternal suffering (compare the suggestion that God suffers the consequences of his own creative endeavours). Fernandez's objection to all of these is not that they don't have validity but that they repeatedly obscure the one explanation which people need and which is of over-whelming practical importance: it is above all the poor, not God, who suffer and their suffering is due mainly not to natural but to political causes. The task is not to encourage passivity by suggesting that the present historical situation can in any way be justified, but to find out who is responsible for it and bring the situation to an end. By implication 'theodicy' is at best a distraction and at worst a hindrance to the real task of theology, which is to work with God on the side of the poor.

Andrew Sung Park is a Korean theologian originally from the North of the country but now living and writing in the US. In *The Wounded Heart of God* he discusses suffering at some length, including the suffering of his own family and the *minjung*, the 'down-and-out' of Korea. The scale of it is enormous. It does not, however, appear to raise any serious problems for his faith in a good God. Suffering or HAN (an Asian concept) is the pain of the victim. It can be defined as 'the critical wound of the heart generated by unjust psychosomatic repression, as well as by social, political, economic, and cultural oppression'.[25] It is caused by human sin. In turn it provokes a sense of sin and sin itself as the victim gives way to resentment and hatred, for example, and seeks revenge, often in unjust ways. This is what Park calls 'original HAN': the inherited pain which provokes us to sin but for which we are not responsible.[26] Suffering and its causes are therefore complex, but it is rooted in human perversity. Beyond that any ultimate cause or reason for it is not discussed. Theodicy as such is therefore set aside. God also suffers HAN. Wounded by sin, God suffers because of the oppressor and suffers with the oppressed. Difficult questions about God's responsibility for suffering, whether proactive or permissive, are not addressed. Abstract concepts like omnipotence and omniscience are not regarded as helpful. They have little meaning and do not add to the knowledge of God. At this level once again we apparently do not know. What is much more meaningful is God's suffering with the oppressed of history. He is not known by way of a somewhat detached and objective intellectual discussion or 'orthodoxy', certainly not by that alone[27] but by way of sharing with him in the suffering of the downtrodden. Once again it is our experience of God which counts.

Christian theology, according to Park, has paid too much attention to sin and to the sinners who cause the suffering of HAN, fashioning doctrines of atonement which offer them forgiveness. It has paid too little attention to the suffering of the victims.[28] Any satisfactory way forward will have to deal with both. Justification by faith must coincide with justice for the victims of history. Sin has to be forgiven, both the sin of the oppressor and the vengeful sin of the victim, but the suffering it causes has to be addressed just as urgently, if not more so, and the victims have to be involved in the process of mutual transformation.

In this way Park does not so much direct our theological attention and energy away from theodicy (he tends to side-step its questions) as from our preoccupation with sin and atonement: 'the issue of HAN has been more significant in my life than the problem of sin. Accordingly, my theological theme has been how to resolve the human suffering which wounds the heart of God'.[29] Nevertheless, Park reinforces the practical thrust of both African and other Asian writers towards the tasks of liberation or orthopraxis identifying, as God does, with the poor (downtrodden) and their struggles; and a substantial part of his book is devoted to the practical steps which need to be taken.

Gustavo Gutiérrez of Peru is the father of liberation theology. He tackles the problem of theodicy in his commentary: *On Job: God-talk and the Suffering of the Innocent.*[30] His distinction between the 'evil of guilt', much discussed in the West, and the 'evil of misfortune', much neglected according to Gutiérrez, echoes Park's distinction between 'sin' and 'HAN'. Suffering is once again not exceptional but overwhelming. It is deep and boundless. People suffer everywhere.[31] The question is not how to speak of God 'after Auschwitz' but how to do so while suffering of similar and even greater enormity is still going on:

> . . . in Latin America we are still experiencing every day the violation of human rights, murder, and the torture that we find so blameworthy in the Jewish holocaust of World War II . . . . the starvation of millions . . . discrimination against women, especially women who are poor . . . the exiles and the refugees . . . and the corpse-filled common graves of Ayacucho. What we must deal with is not the past but, unfortunately, a cruel present and a dark tunnel with no apparent end . . . How are we to speak of the God of life when cruel murder on a massive scale goes on in 'the corner of the dead'?[32]

The key for Gutiérrez is the relationship between 'justice and gratuitousness'.[33] What is clear or becomes clear to Job in his dialogues with his friends and with God, is that Job's own suffering and the suffering of the poor cannot be accounted for within the narrow confines of any theory of retributive justice. It is a framework of merits and demerits, worthiness and unworthiness which God explicitly rejects as a basis for his dealings with us. What is behind his behaviour and gives it meaning is not a justice system of rewards and punishments but God's free and unmerited love, often described by Gutiérrez as 'gratuitous' love. In contrast to a confining logic of retribution and reward, the free love of God is unfettered by any logic at all. It could be said that God is more than just. Here Gutiérrez refers to the parables of the workers in the vineyard (Matt. 20) some of whom came late to the job but were paid a full day's wage, and of the prodigal son (Luke 15) who got a homecoming out of all proportion to what he deserved. It is this same love which is behind God's creation and his partiality for the poor and oppressed. He does not show his special concern for them because they are necessarily morally superior to their oppressors. It is not a reflection of what they deserve but of God's love, free of any quid pro quo constraints.

The fact that God does not deal with us according to what we deserve but according to his love does not, however, qualify in the least his desire and demand for justice for the innocent sufferer, for the weak and the oppressed. Both words must therefore be spoken about God, and when Job comes to understand this towards the end of the dialogues, he ceases to complain about God. He repents of his dust and ashes. In other words, he stops grumbling and cheers up. God, he now sees, acts according to his gratuitous love and has a plan 'that cannot be contained in the straitjacket of the doctrine of retribution'.[34] But God also demands justice. The two go together: justice and the unconfined gratuitous love which breaks its bounds and is more than just.

If for Job and for Gutiérrez this amounts to a satisfactory theodicy at the experiential level where Job (like Young) confronts God face to face: not hearing of him with the ear but seeing him with the eye, it seems curiously unsatisfactory at the level of theological reflection. If it explains God's preference for the poor, it hardly explains their poverty. At worst it could appear to suggest that innocent suffering is subsumed within a loving plan of God which is superior to or unconstrained by Job's orderly, retributive justice. What Job complained of as being in fact worse than retributive justice – of a lower moral order because it was undeserved – is now to be regarded as part of a higher order; which would seem to be a decidedly perverse conclusion to draw. God may deal with us in ways that are more than just, but innocent suffering on a horrific scale can hardly be one of them.

At best Job's and Gutiérrez's faith in both God's love and God's justice gives up the attempt to produce any kind of rationale for suffering. It is not fairly distributed as punishment for sin; neither is it part of the necessary conditions for soul-making (compare Hick) or for human freedom (compare Young). There is no knowing or theological guessing what it is. One can only contemplate the unconfined and unrestricted love of God as Job encounters him and as Christians encounter him in Christ, a love which, as 'gratuitous', is by definition inexplicable. The contemplation of such love does not obscure suffering and it does not explain it; but neither does suffering cancel that love out.

One is left with the prophetic drive towards justice. God desires it and God demands it, and whilst our recognition of his love does nothing to help us understand why the innocent suffer it does undergird and cleanse our understanding of justice. God does not seek justice for the poor and oppressed, or require us to seek it, out of any consideration for what they do or do not deserve. Too much talk of innocence and blame, of merits and rights, is out of place and clouds the issue. God seeks justice for the poor simply because God loves them. It is a gratuitous love: free of any explanation, unconstrained by reason or logic, including the logic of retribution for the wicked or reward for the innocent or more deserving.

7. Some conclusions about theodicy

We have seen how, in their different ways, a number of theologians of the 'South', of Africa, Asia and South America, whilst discussing the issues of poverty and oppression as they confront the horrific 'normality' of suffering, tend not to engage in theodicy as such. They make little attempt to explain suffering beyond stating that it is the result of sin. They do not try to reconcile it with either the permissive or proactive love of God. They only reassert God's determination to be rid of it and free his children from it. They may not turn out to be wholly representative, but what conclusions might be drawn from this apparent neglect of theodicy in the South in marked contrast to the continuing attempts of theologians in the North, including, for example, the vast corpus of writing on the subject that John Hick alone has inspired, to give a more satisfying account of how evil is compatible with the existence of a God who is both good and powerful?

First, it is comparatively easy to announce 'the end of theodicy': to herald its demise. It is apparent that all theodicies are *unsuccessful*; but that is not necessarily a criticism. They are bound to be unsuccessful and those who venture on them know it well. Despite our growing knowledge, and highly revealing events like the life and death of Jesus that increase our understanding, the universe remains profoundly mysterious. We don't know far more than we do know. The only legitimate target for criticism would be a theodicy which is less thoughtful or 'successful' than it needs to be or, worse, a theodicy which works all too well amongst those for whom suffering is not a problem only because their accounts of it are shallow and cruelly misleading.

Second, like all theology, theodicy is *contextual*, which may partly explain why it is pursued by some more than others, by the 'North', for example, more than by the 'South'. It is interesting to note that in this instance it is apparently pursued far less urgently by those who suffer than by those who don't. We might have expected the reverse to be true. The contrast, however, between the deeply religious culture of Africa, where the exist-ence of God is unselfconsciously assumed as a fact of everyday life, and the more secular culture of Europe, where God's exist-ence has to be argued for and his reputation defended, may be one contextual reason why theodicy, as an exercise in apolo-getics, receives more attention in the North.[35] There is a rather different agenda to be addressed.

Third, continuing hard work on theodicy is *defensible* on at least two grounds. It can be positively supportive of the Christian believer: easing some of the pain and offence caused by suffering, removing unnecessary doubts and hesitations which might demotivate co-operation with God, and releasing energies for the tasks of faith. It can also be seen as part of the creative task described by Vanstone. Suffering, as disordered chaos, has no meaning. We shall not, therefore, set out to find the hidden meaning within it or point it out to others as a way of offering them comfort. It isn't there. Suffering has no meaning. We may, however, give it meaning. We may bring to it some kind of order, bend and use it to some good purpose. We may put it in better shape and try to 'make' something of it as, for example, the Irenaean tradition, favoured by Hick, encourages us to do. God may not have designed suffering into his plans as a tool for soul-making, but we may turn it around and even in this, as in all things, work together with God for good.

Fourth, theodicy may be *suspect* as well as defensible. The 'end' or aim of theodicy is ambiguous. Motives are, as ever, mixed. Whilst it can be supportive and encouraging, consciously or unconsciously it can remove the offence of suffering. It has a tendency to justify the status quo. It can encourage acquiescence and resignation. It can make suffering seem more acceptable than it ever ought to be, sometimes crudely and blatantly so. Theodicy then has more to do with 'maintenance' than with 'mission', and the cynical discipline of 'hermeneutical suspicion' may well need to be brought into play. Whose interests are being served? Theodicy may not only comfort those who mourn and wonder why on earth this should happen to them, it may also be highly convenient teaching for those who don't suffer all that much and prefer the world to stay more or less as it is.

Finally, given the famine of 1984 from which we began and the global reality of poverty and suffering, its enormity and 'normality', theodicy should be a *secondary priority* as a theological pursuit. The task, following Marx, is to understand the world in order to change it, not to explain it in order to justify it, and the resources and efforts of theological reflection should be spent mainly on tackling the question: 'How is the world with all its suffering to be changed for the better?', rather than on asking: 'How is all the suffering of the world to be understood?' That is the real steer given to us by the theologians of the South, pointing us towards the conclusion, to which we shall return, that theology and Christianity should be judged on several grounds but above all according to whether or not they contribute to historical change in favour of the poorest. Such a sense of priorities in our theological endeavours and such a criterion to measure them by may well be in line with the bias of the gospel and with God's preferential option for the poor.

So if I stay with theodicy, it will be because it can be supportive of our vocation to bring good news to the poor. If we turn away from it, it is not primarily because it will inevitably fail, as it will, for as long as we don't know everything, or because it can be used for questionable ends or purposes, defending the indefensible, but because theology has more important things to do: informing the task of liberation and learning, maybe with God as much as from God, how to turn famine into fasting and feasting, and poverty and suffering into detachment and joy.

2

THE IMPACT OF
CHRISTIANITY

1. The flood

On a summer's day in the late 1980s I attended a conference at
Lancaster House in London of government officials, politicians,
civil engineers, environmentalists and representatives of aid and
development agencies to discuss the problems of Bangladesh,
one of the poorest countries in the world. Above all we met to
find a blueprint for putting an end to its disastrous floods.

Not all flooding in Bangladesh is disastrous. Much of it, like
the flooding of the Nile, spells life, irrigating the rice fields and
often making possible more than one crop a year. The water can
be difficult to handle but it has been largely tamed. High roads
are built above the water level. High banks and deep ditches
channel it. Sluices and flood gates control it. Ponds and
reservoirs contain it. Simple pumping systems using appropriate
technology lift it and pour it over the ground. Ingenious floating
hen houses, like miniature Noah's arks, allow the chickens to ride
it. Travellers cross it on crowded ferry-boats. Even when the
water overflows the difficulties it creates can be met with a smile,
like that of the fish farmer as he proclaimed the benefits of a 'free-
market' economy when, in the rising flood waters, fish escaped
from other people's ponds for him to catch and eat free, gratis
and for nothing. And when the water overflows rather too much,
local people have grown adept at mounting their own emergency
operations which have proved superior on more than one

occasion to the high-tech and heavy-handed approaches of outside agencies.

But in 1988, for example, disaster struck. The waters covering the earth must have seemed almost as universal and destructive to the inhabitants of Bangladesh as they did to the people of Mesopotamia in the days of Noah. Millions lost their houses or sat helpless on their rooftops. Animals were washed away. Crops were lost. Thousands of people died. Almost everyone went hungry. Typhoid and cholera and all manner of diseases were rife. An international operation for relief and rehabilitation was mounted and a massive emergency appeal went out for money to pay for it. The conference in London was organized to find a modern counterpart to the rainbow in the ancient Mesopotamian sky: a promise that such a disaster would not happen again (Gen. 9.12–17).

Part of the solution was long-term, as most 'final' solutions are. The flooding could not be traced to 'natural' or, for that matter 'divine', causes. Bangladesh was the victim of increasing environmental neglect from below and above. From below, the islands of low-lying land around the Bay of Bengal were being overwhelmed by the sea, probably because neglect of the ozone layer was causing global warming and the sea levels to rise. From above, the Indian mountains to the north were losing their trees so that instead of holding and checking the flow of water it rolled down uncontrolled. So the seas rose and the rivers burst their banks and the floods covered the face of the known earth. The immediate proposals of the Lancaster House conference involved massive engineering works: widening, deepening and diverting rivers and canals to carry away the excess water.

In 1991 and 1998 Bangladesh suffered yet more disasters from cyclone and flood. The new measures had failed to check the destructive waters. Life and death went on much as before and I experienced not just deep disappointment but the stirrings of another challenge to my Christian faith as undermining as my encounter with famine in the Horn of Africa in 1987.

It would be easy to argue that the challenge was ill-founded. The recurrence of the flood had little, if anything, to do with Christianity or matters of faith. It was a matter for technicians, not believers. It had to do with the fact that the longer-term environmental measures, such as extensive reforestation, had not and could not have been completed between one great flood and the next; and even if they had it was too early for them to take effect. It was also due to the fact that the engineering works were not complete or radical enough or agreed to by all the interested parties. In some respects they were simply misconceived. True, there could have been a lack of will, even goodwill, and of the generosity that was needed to make available the necessary resources – matters which might be regarded as more directly related to a Christian agenda – but the main lessons to be learned were entirely practical. What was required was a better scheme and a more co-ordinated effort to implement it.

It was this flood, however, justifiably or not, and the 'rainbow' of promises which turned out to be no guarantee against disaster, which awakened my unease, and they readily and quickly gathered round them ample evidence to suggest that this unease was justified. The flood became a parable of so much else: a parable of how the world does not change fundamentally but goes on much the same as before. In Bangladesh flood follows flood. In the Horn of Africa the survivors went back to their land after the 1984 'famine'. Rehabilitation programmes provided them with seeds and tools. The rains came. Crops were harvested. Peace was made between Ethiopia, Tigré and Eritrea. War ceased to aggravate poverty. Reforestation programmes set out to green the land. Several quite serious crop failures occurred, but due to much better arrangements for food storage and distribution few people died from hunger. But by 1998 Ethiopia and Eritrea were at war again and in 1999 and again in January 2000 came reports of a 'famine' in the Horn of Africa likely to be even more devastating than the 'famine' of 1984–85.

In the mid-1940s, to take another example, the churches in

Europe joined together in an ecumenical partnership to recon-
struct their lives and their church buildings after the war. More
importantly, they united to rebuild the lives of the refugees
the war had left behind. They resolved to deal with the refugee
problem once and for all: a 'final solution' of a benevolent kind.
Having dealt with Europe, they then turned their attention to
refugees in Palestine and from there to displaced and dispossessed people across the world. Their humanitarian strategy
gradually became clear. They would deal immediately with emergency situations, including the plight of refugees and victims of
'natural' disasters, but they would not allow emergency relief
work to distract their attention from the main task of longer-term
sustainable development whereby poor communities would be
supported in tackling their problems in a more permanent way.
They were determined not only to treat the symptoms but to cure
the disease; not just to ease the pain but to remove its causes.

Fifty years later two stark facts cannot be gainsaid. First, the
number of refugees has multiplied and the problem has become
more and more complex. The complexity is reflected in a
lengthening vocabulary which now speaks not only of refugees
but of homeless people, economic migrants, the uprooted,
asylum seekers and more. As to their numbers, there are believed
to be more refugees in the world than ever; and more refugees in
Europe – in the Balkans and elsewhere – than there were in the
mid-1940s.

The second undeniable fact is the growing number of
disaster situations: famine, flood (not only in Bangladesh but in
Central America in 1998 and 1999 and Mozambique in 2000, for
example), earthquake, tempest (in Orissa on the east coast of
India and in the Bay of Bengal in 1999, for example) and conflict.
They all place huge demands on humanitarian agencies: their
time, energy and money. The issues they raise threaten to domi-
nate their agendas. Instead of gradually giving way to long-term
development, disasters and emergency relief aid become a major
preoccupation.

The world does not seem to change all that much and the bleak catalogue of evidence is easily enlarged. In 1980, for example, more than twenty years ago, Willy Brandt's *North–South* report on world poverty[1] famously put its finger on the need to reverse the relentless flow of resources from South to North. They still flow, just as relentlessly, roughly in the same wrong direction, not least in debt repayments, and the gap between rich and poor still grows. In 1989 the Cold War came to an end but it was followed by an escalation of conflict in many countries, especially Africa. (At a church service in November 1999, I heard a woman pray for peace in thirty-four conflict situations.) The Holocaust was finally and universally condemned, since when genocide has been perpetrated in Rwanda, in Bosnia and Kosovo and in East Timor, and they are only the more public examples of communal murder, rape and pillage.

Once a measure of disappointment has set in at the failure to deal with poverty and suffering over the past fifty to sixty years, as it did for me when faced with the recurrence of disastrous floods in Bangladesh, it is hard to prevent it colouring our whole historical perspective. My own view is that history confronts us with what I would describe as an 'unstable stable state'. There is no need and no wish to deny that good has been achieved, indeed to do so would be to fly in the face of the very experiences we try to take seriously in the pastoral cycle of reflecting on practice. UN statistics on poverty show a marked decline in infant mortality rates and marked improvements in the numbers of children going to school, the availability of healthcare and clean water to drink. In Bangladesh relatively simple development programmes like fish ponds, women's co-operatives and credit schemes improve the quality of people's lives. Similar stories can be told about many other countries. On a larger scale, popular opinion has been mobilized in the last few years by the Jubilee 2000 campaign to cancel unsustainable international debts. It has forced itself on the attention of some of the world's most powerful governments and financial institutions. It has achieved a substantial reduction in the burden of debt in some of the world's poorest nations. In South Africa apartheid was brought to an end.

But what is gained, as we have seen, can be lost. What is promised may not be realized. New problems arise to take the place of the old, as if evil as well as nature abhors a vacuum. Oppression and indifference do not go away. The flood and the famine return. New mechanisms of control and exploitation are found to replace debt – just as debt replaced slavery. Economic apartheid strangles the poor where political apartheid has loosened its grip. A great deal of change takes place and not just of the scenery. History is an 'unstable' state. There is real movement and often for good. But experience and hindsight suggest that overall the level of our moral and spiritual achievements, of our humanity and inhumanity, remains 'stable' and much the same as ever it was.

2. The biblical promise

What then is to become of a faith – my faith – which is full of the promise of historical change for the better? The promise runs through the Old Testament. Abraham will have a son in his old age and become the father of a great nation. The Israelites under Moses will be set free from slavery in Egypt and journey towards the land of Canaan where they will drive out their enemies and settle in peace and plenty. Exiles in Babylon will return home. Jerusalem will be rebuilt and restored to its proper standing among the nations. Those who wait for the Messiah will see God's salvation prepared before the face of all the peoples. Second Isaiah (chapters 40–55) offers an astonishingly promising scenario.

Admittedly this vision of historical change for the better is a narrow one. It focusses on the fortunes of one nation which finds it more and more difficult under the pressures of misfortune to remember its calling to be a servant and to be the means by which all the nations of the earth will bless themselves. But the vision was soon broadened by some of the Old Testament prophets and radically so when the Messiah came. Many of the old assumptions were then thrown into disarray. The promised Kingdom was not quite like anything they had imagined. They were forced to re-think its character, its membership, and the manner of its coming. And it was more inclusive than anything they had expected. But when the dust settled and they realized that history itself was not about to come to an end, this great Christian enterprise inaugurated by Jesus and elaborated by Paul and John and other leaders of the early church was clearly going to change the world. It would fulfil the promises of Isaiah (Mark 1.2). Evil would be overcome; sinners would be transformed; the poor would be lifted high; sickness would be cured; demons driven away; reconciliation would break out between men and women, Jew and Gentile; the principalities and powers of this world would be brought to heel; there would be nothing less than a new heaven and a new earth. The cost of it all would be great, but it was a cost that love was prepared to bear and it would win through. Christianity would redeem and recreate the world.

In recent years 'impact studies' have become the vogue in development circles. Those who provide the financial resources, particularly governments, have become increasingly interested in how their money is spent and whether it is spent effectively. Those involved in development, especially the so-called 'beneficiaries', have also quite rightly wanted to evaluate their work and where possible learn from their successes and mistakes in order to do even better. Measuring the impact of development programmes is far from easy. For one thing, it is difficult to isolate cause and effect. Many interrelated factors are always involved and any particular 'input' or contribution may or may not be the reason for the observed outcome. For another thing, development is a moving picture where ideas change in the light of experience and objectives are reconsidered. Setting out to achieve one thing, a community may end up wishing to achieve another.

The goal posts get moved. So impact studies don't easily come up with answers. They are judged worth doing, nevertheless.

Christianity has had an incalculable impact on history. Without it the world as we know it would be unrecognizable. It has profoundly affected religious, social, cultural, political and economic life. Hardly anything remains untouched. That is not, however, the point. In development the point is to see whether what we set out to achieve is achieved or not. Did we put an end to famine and flood, to debt and conflict, to uprootedness and disease? And if not, then why not?

Christianity apparently set out to redeem the times and make a new world, or maybe make or create a world for the very first time. It would bring in the Kingdom. Any impact study looks almost certain to suggest that it has failed to do so, and that triggers off in me a severe challenge to my faith. I begin to wonder whether Christianity's claim to change the world for good is misplaced or even false, since it has manifestly failed to live up to its promises, leaving the poor where they always were which is anywhere but on the thrones of the mighty.

But, as in the case of the famine of 1984, before such scepticism takes hold as little more than an emotional reaction to a particular experience, we had better try to steady and deepen it by reflection. We had better ask why? Why has Christianity had little or no impact on history perceived as an 'unstable stable state'? Why has it been so unredemptive and uncreative overall?

3. Sin

The most obvious reply is because our stubborn and recalcitrant human wills oppose it at every turn. Sin is always at the door and its roots are to be found in a kind of wilful or gratuitous disobedience which refuses to co-operate with God only, apparently, because it chooses not to, engaging instead in mindless rebellion just for the sake of it. We are simply perverse.

In Rwanda in 1994, not long after the genocide, I had sat and listened to pastors and church leaders discussing the way forward and calling for repentance and reconciliation. Their sombre and well-meaning recipe for peace was based on precisely these assumptions which also provide the background to many theories of atonement and frequent offers of divine forgiveness. The men and women of Rwanda, Hutus and Tutsis, were the guilty parties. They had chosen to kill for no good reason. They should now turn round and choose to do otherwise. But the recipe did not convince me, given the history and the cruel circumstances that weighed against these people. The assumption that sin is rooted in perversity sounded hollow and, with it, the suggestion that the same persistent perversity accounts for the failure of Christianity.

To be fair, Christian teaching about human sin is highly sophisticated. It does not, for example, heap inordinate blame on individuals. It is acutely aware that although they aggravate their sinful condition, it is largely not of their own making. There is 'original sin'. The problem is inherited. The sins of the fathers are visited on the children to the third and fourth generation and well beyond that. One thing leads to another. Destructive behaviour creates suffering and suffering or HAN[2] provokes destructive behaviour. 'Original HAN' adds to the darkness and makes matters worse. Given the past and the present into which we are born, we are down (sinful) before we have fallen (sinned). So to talk about sin and demand repentance and reconciliation is not to make a crude and cruel accusation that those immediately involved, like the brutalized killers of Rwanda, are entirely to blame for what they do. The accursed situation is bigger than they are.

And if sinners are not entirely to blame, neither are they expected to find their own way out unaided. Christian teaching accepts that, left to themselves, sinners cannot repent and achieve reconciliation. Christianity has much to say about salvation by faith and not by works, and it has even more to say about grace. Help is at hand. There are resources above and beyond our own, so that to call for repentance is not to make an unreasonable demand of those who are physically, mentally and spiritually exhausted and morally bankrupt, or to leave them to haul themselves up by their own bootstraps and solve their own problems. Christianity shows constraint in not heaping too much responsibility, for good or for ill, on our contemporary shoulders.

At least four other important insights are safeguarded by understanding sin as wilful perversity. The first is that human beings are not mere puppets controlled by outside forces with no strings to pull of their own. They are not wholly determined. They can rise above their circumstances. To a limited extent they are free. Second, if they are capable of making the wrong choice, they are capable of making the right one. 'Free' means 'free'. Their decision can go either way including the way of selfless generosity and creative endeavours. To deny that we are guilty is also to deny that we can make a constructive contribution towards turning a tragic situation around. There is a silver lining to the dark cloud of our propensity for doing evil. Calling people 'sinners' is a backhanded way of acknowledging them as responsible human beings. Third, Christian teaching about sin is determined to call a spade a spade. Appalling acts of cruelty and unkindness are not to be explained away or allowed to die the death of a thousand excuses. The evil that we do is not merely the consequence of some upsetting experiences or an unfortunate background that we could do nothing about. Whatever else needs to be said, neighbours savaged neighbours in Rwanda as they do in many a conflict situation. Genocide occurred. Evil was done and that given fact is not altered by the circumstances in which it occurred. A fourth insight has been underlined by Eleazar Fernandez and other theologians in their discussions about theodicy or how our belief in a good God can be reconciled with human suffering or, rather, in their hesitations about too many discussions of that kind. The risk is that they may turn the spotlight away from what should remain the focus of attention. The reality of suffering, including the causes of poverty and injustice, may be obscured by fatalism or too much talk about the mystery of it all or by thoughtful speculation about its inevitability or necessity if we are to find our true selves and the way to God. The more relevant fact for these Southern theologians is that suffering, including war and flood, is of our making. It is a human construct: 'a product of history and a creation of people'.[3] It is the result of political decisions, for example, not theological mysteries, and if such decisions can be made, they can be undone.

For all that, it still seems mistaken to explain our stubborn opposition to God's creative work fundamentally in terms of sinful perversity: strip away history and circumstance and at the core lies mindless rebellion against God. In effect that is no explanation at all since it offers no reason as to why, to use the language of myth, given Paradise, we would set out to destroy it or, unless provoked in some way, seek to rise disastrously above our station.

It seems more sensible to assume that the roots of our opposition to God, or rather of our highly destructive behaviour which continually frustrates God's redemptive and creative purposes, are to be found in our insecurity rather than our perversity.[4] It is because we don't feel safe, both inwardly and outwardly, and fear for ourselves that we engage in behaviour which is egotistic, self-regarding rather than other regarding, and in often misguided attempts to protect ourselves physically and emotionally as individuals and as groups. Poor and rich are alike in this respect, whether they are the tribes of Rwanda or the Balkans or the comfortable majorities of democracies. All act to safeguard their own interests, although they do it in different ways, and in so doing they breed discord, oppression and pain rather than a reconciled humanity.

The cause of this insecurity may be a problem for God, as we shall see. God may yet have to learn how to deal with it. It may, however, be the result of God's deliberate choice, since God is surely quite capable of making his goodness and his love for us so overwhelmingly plain and his presence so real that all thoughts of insecurity would disappear and we would happily fall into line? The result, however, would be men and women who had no choice but to love God and that would be no real love at all. God's love would be irresistible. They would have no space to be themselves or make up their own minds. So God keeps God's distance. God woos but does not overwhelm. God's presence remains ambiguous, not obvious; and the opposition is necessarily given its head.

The inconclusive nature of all theodicy comes back again, however, to haunt us. Previously[5] we objected to this argument in support of the unnerving absence of God on the grounds that God's infinite resourcefulness was surely capable of devising more effective ways of wooing his creatures without overwhelming them. If God is to win us in the 'end', and must one day be more resourceful and successful in doing so, why not now? Faced with the flood we can put the objection more bluntly. Whether it amounts to wilful perversity or insecurity, if God's redemptive enterprise is frustrated because of our continuing sinful opposition, that only underlines how ineffective it is in dealing with the very reality it sets out to redeem. What are we to make of a gospel which claims to rescue sinners but has little impact on their sinful and destructive behaviour? It looks like impotence.

4. Principalities and Powers

Some contemporary writing, notably that of Walter Wink,[6] suggests that the failure of Christianity is due not just to the opposition but to the strength of the opposition: to the 'Principalities and Powers' of this world. It draws our attention to a whole dimension of 'sin' which we have failed to take account of adequately or to understand.

The opposing forces are not sinful individuals. They are corporate realities, and it is not hard to think of possible examples in the struggle against poverty, though we must be careful not to write them off as unambiguously evil. They would include International Financial Institutions such as the World Bank, the International Monetary Fund and the World Trade Organization. They were originally designed to assist the economic development of poorer countries through aid, investment and trade, but in recent years they have often been sharply criticized for sacrificing the interests of the poor in the name of a stubborn allegiance to a 'free-market', capitalist system which mainly benefits the rich. Alongside them is the G7 (or 8) uniting the interests of the richest and most powerful nations on earth. Other 'Powers' would be the huge transnational companies whose turnover is greater than the GNP (Gross National Product) of many poorer countries put together, and whose influence can be greater than that of the nation state. Transnational corporations gain access to markets which the state might well wish to protect and they are left free to move their capital across borders at will and to speculate rather than invest. They can be a law unto themselves. These corporate 'Powers' are also found within countries as well as beyond and around them, in the hierarchical and oppressive systems of class and caste, race and religion.

The origin of the 'Powers' is sometimes located in stories about fallen angels where the sheer perversity of supernatural beings replaces the sheer perversity of men and women. Such tales are not only unhelpful but unnecessary since it is comparatively easy to see how in their insecurity people group together to protect and promote what they believe to be their interests and how one thing then leads to another. Wink describes the doctrine of the Fall and its mythical language as 'merely a mute pointer' to what he calls the 'sludge' or 'sedimentation of thousands of years of human choices';[7] in other words it is the accumulation of protective moves which have negative effects but are human and understandable nevertheless.

But there are two features of these 'Powers' which do make them, as it were, 'larger than life'. First, the sum of them is greater than their parts. They take on a life of their own. They are difficult to control. Those who belong to them typically wonder as to where power lies. Those who are supposed to rule over them typically despair of translating their policies into practice. They are complex and wilful organisms to manage. People get caught up in what is far bigger than themselves.

Second, the 'Powers' are not just flesh and blood. Wink points to what he calls the 'interiority' of institutions. This is not simply a reference to organizational culture or atmosphere or esprit de corps. It is more proactive and self-conscious. Just as an individual is to be understood and treated as a psychosomatic unity with a body and a soul, so are transnational corporations and the like. They have inner, wilful spirits. They have 'angels'; and just as we have turned in on ourselves and fallen away from our true vocation to love and to serve, so have they.

The lack of success in transforming the Powers for good is due therefore, amongst other things, to a failure to recognize what we are dealing with. We look at capitalism, for example, only as if it were an economic system: a body without a soul. We assume we can correct its tendencies to maintain and exacerbate the gap between rich and poor and enhance its potential for creating and distributing wealth and opportunity by devising new economic mechanisms and systems. We will adjust the working machinery. We will introduce, for example, new forms of taxation and global governance. We will reorganize its institutions. Meanwhile we ignore the 'spirit of capitalism'. We fail to recognize the need for repentance or a change of heart and mind. It does not occur to us to convert this enormous institution to a different set of values and commitments and if it did, we would scarcely know where to start.

Which takes us to another possible response to the apparent failure of Christianity. Perhaps it is wrong to judge it as if it were a perfectly knowledgeable instrument of redemption and creation. If it is a mistake to regard redemption and creation as in any way complete and God in Christ as having already redeemed us, it may also be wrong to regard redemption and creation as a completely assured process which knows exactly what to do next. What we have instead is a God like Christ, utterly committed to redeeming the times, bringing good news to the poor, fashioning an ordered and hospitable world out of chaos, giving meaning to a void of suffering which has no meaning, drawing us into the enterprise but learning as we go, God and us together, and often painfully as false moves bring unforeseen consequences and compound the difficulties. If the impact of Christianity is far from impressive, it is because it does not exactly know how to transform the earth but is busy discovering how, including how to convert the 'Powers' that all too often overwhelm us and seem to be beyond our reach.

This is a very attractive suggestion. It accords well with many experiences in development. Forlorn attempts at flood control was one of them. My own encounter with the first and second green revolutions in Sri Lanka was another. The first revolution brought high-yielding seeds and abundant crops. It was a great step forward. It seemed to achieve its aim of providing enough good food for everyone. But there were problems. Fresh seeds had to be bought in each year. They needed fertilizers and pesticides. Agrobusiness in the form of powerful transnational corporations controlled supplies and put up prices. The first revolution eventually became too expensive with Third World farmers once again far too dependent on the outside world. A second green revolution was announced. Some referred to it as 'organic farming', as if it were something new. It was, in fact, a return to many of the old ways. Locally produced seeds were used instead of the newer patented varieties. Mixed crops controlled the pests. Natural fertilizers replaced the chemicals. All in all, it represented a fresh appreciation of the wisdom of traditional methods for all their limitations. It was a learning process. Co-operatives, to take another example, which unlike the techniques of farming are more psychosomatic in character, having a corporate organization or body and an interior spirit, seem to throw up as many problems as they solve. It still proves difficult to harness the energy that more readily goes into private enterprise to these shared endeavours for the common good and get people to work as hard in the shared field with its economies of scale as they do on their own small plots of land.

So there is much we do not know and have yet to learn about how to turn things round and make them better. But such modesty does not let Christianity entirely off the hook. The impact study may still come up with a disappointing result. If it now claims not to be redemptive and creative but to be committed to learning how to redeem and create, then Christianity's record as a pupil seems remarkably poor. It is certainly not in the 'A' stream. If it has not failed the test because it has failed to redeem, it has failed because it has failed to learn.

5. Progress

But perhaps in all of this we are over-influenced by relatively recent ideas of progress. Is it too simplistic to suggest that until the early eighteenth century Christians found themselves in a fairly static world in any case? Things went on much the same from year to year, century to century, and were not expected to do otherwise. The Enlightenment, which questioned the old authorities and their settled views, and the dawn of empirically-based knowledge and science, which swept away old mysteries and gave us a greater sense of control, began to change all of that. In fact the spectacular success of science with its rapidly growing catalogue of inventions made it reasonable to think that all problems could be solved, including the problems of hunger and disease and poverty. The 'Age of Reason' was not without its pessimists. The Lisbon earthquake, for example, was a sobering blow. The novel *Candide* is riddled with cynicism. But in general the world abounded with hope and optimism.

The colonial movements of the next two centuries, including the missionary movement of the churches, and the development movement which followed in their wake, often did more harm than good to those on the receiving end, but they were seen as progressive movements that would change the world. They represented the march of civilization. They would turn darkness to light. The missionaries even expected to rally all the nations to their cause:

> For the darkness shall turn to dawning,
> And the dawning to noon-day bright,
> And Christ's great Kingdom shall come on earth,
> The Kingdom of love and light.

> (Colin Sterne, 1862–1926)

Christian Socialists had progressivist views[8] and as late as the 1950s 'the world for Christ in this generation' was still a slogan used by the Student Christian Movement. Even the grim record of the twentieth century (which the Dalai Lama recently called 'the century of blood') including genocide, growing environmental disaster and persistent exploitation and poverty, has done little to rid us of a sense that history moves on rapidly and more or less in the right direction. Harvey Cox, the secular theologian, once equated the modern city with the Kingdom of God.[9]

This progressive mind-set, fuelled even today by the steep learning curve of science in an age of information technology, can rob us of a sense of historical perspective. Advance for us is speedy and in the short term. We have difficulty in recognizing it in any other form. We overlook the long, long story of gradually emerging forms of life, of their evolving complexities, of the slow rise of humanity to self-consciousness and self-direction and moral sensibility. To judge the redemptive and creative work of love on the basis of the last two thousand years is to take an extremely foreshortened view of history and pre-history. A truer and longer perspective might well conclude not that God with us had not got very far, but that both materially and spiritually we had come a very long way. And what of all the ages still to come?

Frances Young, confronted with the stubborn fact that no

amount of science or love is going to change a severely handicapped son into one who is physically and mentally 'able' in the
conventional sense, also warns against mistaken ideas of progress.[10] Often we look for the wrong kind of progress, such as
increasing our abilities (in the case of the handicapped often
referred to as 'life skills') where it might be preferable to improve
our relationships: to be friends rather than to be clever. Or again
we forget our limitations. Given the best will in the world and
the faith that is supposed to move mountains there are things we
simply cannot do. We cannot finally overcome our frailty or
vulnerability and at the end of our days we shall die.

The assumption, therefore, that in assessing the impact of
Christianity we are looking for a world which is rapidly improv-
ing on all fronts may need challenging. That is not to say we
should rule anything out in the long run. It is certainly not
possible for us to solve all our problems here and now and, when
it comes to our individual responsibilities, we cannot solve all, if
any, of those problems alone or be blamed for the persistence of
some forms of suffering, like mental and physical disability. It is
too much to expect a cure for all ills. The result is unwarranted
feelings of guilt and failure. That is different, however, from
suggesting that given time – a very long time perhaps – and
patience, and growing wisdom and love, they will not and cannot
be overcome. All things are possible. Even death, after all, is to
lose its sting, according to the claims of the New Testament.

We should not rule anything out; but neither should we take
too much comfort from this much longer perspective which,
with hindsight, reveals a dramatic difference between pre-history
and today and a remarkable story of creativity. Even that cannot
entirely deal with the dismal record of Christianity. 'Late in time',
admittedly, 'behold him come, offspring of a virgin's womb'; but
having come, some kind of new initiative has presumably been
taken; a new age has dawned; a further and decisive stage of the
process has been inaugurated; fresh expectations have been
aroused of redemptive and creative forces at work. Against that

background the impact of Christianity, it could still be said, is not impressive.

6. Christianity and history

But despite the promises of the Bible, were we ever really meant to look for the successful completion of the Christian project in history? It might well have been so with the Jewish project, promising a small nation a secure future in a secure land, though that project could hardly be described as a success. But was it ever the case with the Christian project? It may be completed 'beyond' history or 'after' history, but not within history. To think otherwise is to misunderstand.

The New Testament itself and subsequent Christian teaching carefully hedge their bets. Here are three examples.

First, note the paradoxical descriptions of the Kingdom of God, the goal of the Christian enterprise. It is announced as already here, firmly in the present or close at hand; and yet it is in the future. Its coming is to be prayed for and we do not know when it will be: 'It is not for you to know times or seasons which the Father has fixed by his own authority' (Acts 1.7). The Kingdom is also part of our earthly lives. It is among us and within us. It is appropriately described in terms of everyday realities: coins and seeds, housewives, business people, farmers and parents; and yet the Kingdom is not of this world.

Second, through faith in Christ, believers are to be dramatically delivered from sin. The contrast between before and after is like the difference between darkness and light, death and life, blindness and sight; between being forever dissatisfied and never being thirsty again. And having been saved, these same sinners will be sanctified. By their fruits they will be recognized: the fruits of the spirit. They will be perfect as their father in heaven is perfect. But for all that they remain sinners, saved by grace and not by their works, constantly needing to confess their sins and avoid the arrogance of self-righteousness. The saints will need to pray daily for forgiveness: 'forgive our sins as we forgive those who sin against us'.

Third, the church is to be a colony of heaven where the new relationships between God and Christ's people and between people themselves are realized and practised; and where reconciliation and unity between man and woman, slave and free, Jew and Gentile, become a lived experience. The church is the body of Christ. And yet it remains an all-too-human entity. Indeed it would be highly dangerous to think of it otherwise. It is a flawed and fallible institution. It is not identical with the Kingdom of God. It may witness to the gospel, but it cannot claim to embody it. It will always be in need of constant reformation.

We could draw the cynical conclusion that Christianity has rather cleverly put itself beyond the reach of any impact study. It is not exposed to any kind of 'empirical verification'. No evidence can disprove its case. We can always point to 'signs of the Kingdom' and to harbingers and foretastes of what there is to come as demonstrations of Christianity's ability to redeem and create. But the fact that there are plenty of counter-examples which throw doubt on those claims only goes to show not that Christianity has let us down but that the end time is not yet. When the flood returns and the rainbow proves to be something of an empty promise, Christianity has made itself immune to criticism.

To be more constructive, we may simply have got Christianity wrong. The history of our world or this secular age was never intended to be the scene of Christianity's final achievement, and to be confronted by 'an unstable stable state' where things improve but not overall and not in a progressive or sustained way is at one level perfectly satisfactory. An understanding of the world, for example, as a vale of soul-making[11] almost requires it. At the end of the day on this scenario the world has no lasting significance since, once the making of souls and the bringing of sons and daughters to God is complete, the world's job is done. It is a means to an end. Like scaffolding, it can be safely removed once the work has been completed. History does not itself embody the Kingdom. But for as long as it has a role to play the world must, as we have seen, be a place where evil is encountered. If we live in a world which causes no offence to anyone we shall never be provoked into becoming what we are meant to be.

But if continuing imperfections, suffering and catastrophe are necessary – 'necessary evils' in fact if we are to grow up – so are the welcome achievements we sometimes refer to as signs of the Kingdom. Soul-making is not a process in which we are largely passive, knocked into shape as it were by the hard knocks of life. Souls in the making have to be proactive achievers. They must rise to the challenges, overcome the obstacles, tackle the problems, oppose injustice, improve conditions, strive to turn evil into good, learning and maturing as they go. History has to be the arena of hard work and honest endeavour. If evil remains as part of the plot so does our success in occasionally and partially overcoming it. Wheat and tears have to grow together in the same historical field.

There may be a further misunderstanding. Talk of the Kingdom as 'not yet' and not of this world may not be an evasion but a way of saying that what good we do manage to rescue and create in this world is not so vulnerable as the world is and has permanent significance. We are not involved in little more than a passing show or an exercise. History as a vale of soul-making may not last forever, nor the tears that go with it. But after separating the wheat from the tares and winnowing what remains the harvest most definitely will last. Of course we must take evil seriously when we tackle it in the first place or there is neither genuine redemption nor personal growth, but Christianity takes history even more seriously in that it is a genuine workshop in which we struggle to make communities and good relationships and conduct successful experiments in love and justice and enriching the quality of life; and all of these endure. The world as we know it may fade away, but there is real continuity between making Bangladesh a safer and happier place to live in and the burgeoning quality of life in God's eternal Kingdom. Some have likened Christianity's redemptive and creative achievements in this world to bricks and stones which go to build that Kingdom in another place where it silently increases all the time. Some have likened those achievements to memories stored in the mind of God. Whatever is of value is not forgotten and does not go for nothing.

Properly understood, then, Christianity's apparent double-talk, claiming to right all wrongs but not in any straightforward sense, is not a clever attempt to shield it from criticism. An 'unstable stable state' which apparently gets nowhere very fast is not only the occasion of redemption, it is the condition of it. And there is a kind of empirical test after all, as John Hick has explained,[12] even if we have to wait before applying it. One day Christianity will come clean and when it does it will pass the impact test. This often painful and always ambiguous process will in the end demonstrate its ability to make a world and a home for us all.

We might add one other point, old and familiar as it is, which supports the suggestion that to be disillusioned with Christianity and its claims because it apparently underachieves so spectacularly is to misunderstand it. To look for the successful outcome of all its endeavours in history is a gross act of injustice to all those who will never live to see it, an injustice almost greater than the suffering which appears to be a next-to-normal feature of most of their lives. Unless we are to entertain theories of reincarnation, or accept that we live on quite satisfactorily enough in our children and all the other historical realities we help to shape, most human lives will have been little more than a means to an end.

7. The 'success' of Christianity

There remains one further possibility to be considered as we try to come to terms with Christianity's dismal record. It was high-lighted for me by a somewhat cursory (once again) re-reading of theologians from the South.[13] It is the suggestion that the 'unstable stable state' or overall lack of progress in history, which I experienced as a challenge to my faith and described as the failure of Christianity, may not signify its failure at all but its success, since the aim of much of the Christianity which the North has promoted and the South has inherited has been anything but to redeem and create a world for the sake of justice and the poor.

According to these theologians of the South, Christianity has largely been a religion of the powerful ever since it filled a political vacuum in Rome when the old empire fell apart in the fifth century right down to modern times and its intimate relationships with colonialism, missionaries, world development and the globalization of capitalism. It wanted its power and the way it was exercised to remain unchallenged. The social order it established, which was largely favourable to the powerful, was to stay as it was. It therefore developed what Hugo Assmann has called a number of 'alibis'[14] and used them to make the power of Christ (as against the power of the powerful) politically, or we might say, historically, innocuous. Several examples are given, many of them well known.

First comes Christianity's attitude to the poor. It could be acquiescent, persuading itself that this is the way things are. The poor are always with us. Or it could be judgmental. The poor were largely undeserving of anything better. So the response of Christianity was unsympathetic. Punitive measures were often taken against the poor. They were exploited. At best they were treated as the objects of charity.

Second, sin and salvation were reduced to private matters between an individual and God. They were not social concepts. Oppressive systems and structures were not seen as sinful, only the men and women who lived within them. The new life in Christ did not have social implications, and certainly not radical ones, but found expression in private devotion, acts of charity, personal purity and domestic morality.

Third, this Christianity of the powerful subscribed to teaching

Poverty and Christianity

that went back to Augustine's *City of God* and reappeared at the Reformation in talk about two realms or kingdoms which effectively divorced salvation history and the story of the church from secular history and the story of everyday events in the world, including war and flood and famine. It even justified a double standard. The Sermon on the Mount applied to the one realm but not to the other. To quote Míguez Bonino:

> All historical activity is relativized, and eschatology stands as a *caveat* against all political commitment. As a result we seem to get some 'religious' or at least 'suprahistorical' sphere that takes primacy . . . Salvation in the real and strict sense applies to a spiritual, eternal kingdom; only in an emasculated sense does salvation apply to the temporal realm of history. The ideological functionalism of such a scheme is readily apparent.[15]

It could be used as an excuse for leaving history as it was.

Fourth, the real hope of the Christian is an otherworldly hope. The picture is in a vertical rather than a horizontal plane. It has to do with man and God not man and man, with eternity not time, with heaven not earth, with the spiritual rather than the material, with the world to come.

A fifth alibi is an emphasis on the reconciling role of Christ. It was reflected incidentally in the so-called 'Church Theology' sharply criticized by South African and other theologians in the *Kairos Document*.[16] Christ sits above the conflict crying: 'a plague on both or all your houses' and refusing to take sides or be compromised by what is inevitably provisional and far from perfect. Christ looks for peace between the warring parties but without any change in their oppressive relationships. Master and slave are to care for and respect one another. Some christologies, says Assmann, 'offer us a Christ who never takes sides. They are simply ways of concealing the fact that an option for one side has already been made.'[17]

Sixth, the *Kairos Document* also reminded us, of course, of

'State Theology', a theology of convenience to the powers that be which insists that rulers are appointed by God and are to be obeyed.

A final and seventh hiding place is the abstract, self-contained theology of the West as expressed in philosophical teaching about God and in highly technical christologies and doctrines of atonement. It is almost impossible to use it as a resource for 'applied theology'. It is unable to engage with the particularities of history. It does not want to and it does not need to. The abstract story of man's disobedience against God – of its cosmic consequences whereby one act of gratuitous defiance merits eternal retribution, of the need for a perfect divine sacrifice to satisfy God's wrath and pay the price of sin, of the free gift of forgiveness and justification by faith – this abstract, self-contained story can be told without relating it to history at all, and when it is related it does not seem to make much sense. The episodes of the story do not correspond with experienced realities on the ground.

In these and other ways, according to the theologians of the South, Western Christianity has stripped the faith of any historical implications which might conceivably discomfort the powerful. It is this Christianity which is, according to Gutiérrez, unfortunately 'integrated into the prevailing ideology of domination, so that it lends support and cohesiveness to a capitalist society divided into classes'. It justifies 'the social order that serves their interests [i.e., those of the powerful] and maintains their privileged position'. It puts 'the gospel to ideological use so that it may justify a situation which is contrary to its own most elementary demands'.[18]

What, therefore, I had experienced as the failure of Christianity to redeem and transform history in the interests of the poor is in fact the success of Western Christianity in offering redemption to the powerful whilst making sure, consciously or otherwise, that the history of their power and domination remains untouched. Rueben Alves draws what for him is the obvious conclusion:

'saviours of souls' have to be 'transformed into rebuilders of earth'.[19]

8. Conclusion

We have been looking at possible explanations for Christianity's lack of impact on the ills and sins and sorrows it claims to redeem. Is it due to the stubborn nature and size of the opposition? Is it because there is still so much to learn? Are we over-influenced by modern ideas of progress? Have we misunderstood the relation between Christianity and history? Has Christianity been diverted from its liberating task by powerful vested interests? I want to make some concluding remarks mainly about Storytelling.

First, I accept that there is no way of dealing with the problem that is even remotely satisfying if we think only in terms of the history of the world. The more we blame the opposition, including sinful individuals, or the intractable nature of the raw material we have to work with, or the powers that be, or those who wilfully misuse Christianity for their own interests, the more we compound the failure. Christianity simply cannot redeem them. Its impotence is exposed at every turn. Its reputation can only be saved by reference to realities that are suprahistorical. They may be encountered within history or thought of as being around above and beyond it, but they are more than history itself. If Christianity is to succeed and the Kingdom is to come, then the 'end' of the matter is not finally of this world and we have to live with two worlds at once.

We found the same need to refer to suprahistorical realities when we tried to reconcile the evil we found in the world with a powerful and loving God. Theodicy needs suprahistory as well; and, since we may soon be heading in that direction, so does Christian ethics. The moral claim on us to do what is right and good may seem at first to set us free from the need to keep our eyes anywhere else but on the ground. Justifying a vale of soul-making in a time of famine or creating the Kingdom of God out of the flood may require a belief in another realm of existence, but morals and ethics helpfully confine us to our duties in this one: to seeing that the hungry are fed and the waters recede. That is not, however, altogether true. It is hard, for example, to see why we have a duty to do what is right if doing it will not have good results. Why should we do good if good cannot be achieved? And where is it achieved if it is not achieved in this world? Morals like the Christian redemptive and creative enterprise need to succeed and hope of success can only be offered in suprahistorical terms.

'Stories' with a capital 'S' are for me systematic theologies or accounts of what I believe in narrative form. The best 'Story' I know about living with two worlds at once (history and supra-history) is not about a Paradise lost and found, or a good creation marred by sin and then put right again. It is about a long, drawn out, painful and costly process whereby a Christ-like God learns with us how to make a Paradise, or a Kingdom, or a world out of chaos for the very first time. It is accomplished against great odds and by way of many unforeseen mistakes and in the face of the destructive behaviour which our insecurity rather than our sheer perversity provokes. God's absolute commitment to it, as seen in the Christ for whom no cost is too great to bear, is our best hope of its success, since there is little evidence of success within history. This Paradise, which was never lost but is still to be found, will be of another order of existence than our present history. It is suprahistorical. It will, however, only be discovered and created out of all our patient and costly efforts to create it here and now, and as quickly and completely as we can. Nothing less will be important enough to survive. But the fruits of these endeavours, in the growing stature of men and women and improved historical communities of justice and love, sustain-ability and peace, most certainly will survive. Fashioned in this present earthly workshop and admittedly fragmentary, they will be incorporated into the Kingdom of God. The 'unstable stable state' of history which allows for genuine moral and spiritual achievements, but not for any sustained moral and spiritual progress overall, is perfectly compatible with this Story. And it is the best response I know to the challenges presented to my Christian faith by the scale of poverty in the world which I have called its horrible 'normality', and by the persistence of poverty in the face of a Christian movement which explicitly describes itself as well able to redeem it and make all things new.

When I tell this Story, however, I do so with a number of reservations. First, I know it does not entirely hang together. It leaves God, for example, as an amazingly slow learner. It will certainly need a rewrite. But I am not over-troubled by that, because I accept that we shall always 'not know' more than we do know. We walk on the edge of an unending question mark. The universe presents us with a mystery that grows faster than any of our discoveries. We don't know. Only know-alls can tell entirely satisfactory Stories.

My second reservation is more serious. I find even my own Story very hard to believe, or rather I find myself not believing it or not being able to believe just as much and as often as I do believe. The reasons are not only the two experienced challenges to faith I have been describing: the challenges represented almost parabolically by the famine of Ethiopia and the floods of Bangladesh. The reasons may well lie in the fact that I am a child of what they call 'post-Modernity', though like most children I don't entirely understand my parents. Modernity, following the Enlightenment, made its appeal to universal reason or the common-sense ground on which we could all 'know' what we were talking about and on which, if we put our minds to it, we could all agree. Post-Modernity finds that common ground hard to identify. It is struck by the plurality and relativity of all our knowing – and so am I. I am not alarmed by it, but I am impressed by it. I may tell a Story somewhat to my satisfaction, about a Paradise or world in the making, but if I were a different person in a different time and cultural place I think I know that I would tell another Story. And there is no third party to which we can appeal to to arbitrate which is not itself equally conditioned and therefore 'relative'. I find the Story hard to believe because I find it hard to know by what authority I can tell such a likely tale. And my sense of not knowing and having no sure ground on which to stand is not dispelled by any given truths of so-called 'revelation' or by any overwhelming sense that I can leave its truth to the Person who impresses me most in history – or so I've been taught – namely, Jesus of Nazareth. My disbelief leaves me fairly convinced that our theologies tell us a lot about our human needs but little about anything else and that the one and only thing that is crystal clear is the inescapable claim on me of love and justice.

My third reservation has to do with a tendency to reject the Story as often as I accept it on what I can only describe as moral grounds. It may be an intelligent and necessary effort to make sense of things. It may be a proper exercise in apologetics. It may deal with some of the objections to faith. It may even be the necessary ground of ethics themselves; but I am aware that it can also offer us comfort where there should be none. This Story may take the historical struggle for liberation absolutely seriously, but even so it comes close to justifying the unjustifiable simply by explaining it. It enables us to live with it all. It numbs the pain where the pain, at least morally, should perpetually hurt. That might be bad enough, but this temptation to take comfort where there is no comfort to be had has, in the opinion of Southern theologians, as we have seen, turned vicious in the way that suprahistorical stories have been cynically misused not just to comfort but to entrench the powerful and to contradict the very heart of Christianity's good news for the poor.

It would be untrue to say that I don't believe my Story about the creative endeavours of a Christ-like God. At times it is as native to me as any air I breathe. But it would be equally untrue to say that I ever believe it very easily once I think about it. So where do we go from here?

I do not think the answer is to stop telling suprahistorical

Stories or, in other words, stop doing the traditional work of dogmatic and systematic theology, and neither incidentally do the liberation theologians of the South. They are not 'reductionists' in that sense. They do not collapse everything into a flat-earth religion and a single historical struggle despite their grave suspicions of Stories and ideologies. They do, however, have a very strong preference for the practical, historical task of liberating the poor and they apply a sharp corrective to any Christian tradition which spends too much time in its preaching and teaching 'explaining' and justifying the way things are, sometimes in order to keep them that way. The need for such a corrective is the message which comes over emphatically in this quotation from Gustavo Gutiérrez; but it is a corrective:

> Are we, then, talking about reducing the gospel to purely political terms? Are we advocating a 'political reductionism'? Yes, in the case of those who use it to serve the interests of those in power; no, in the case of those who denounce that usage on the basis of its message of liberation and gratuitous divine love. Yes, in the case of those who place themselves and the gospel in the hands of the mighty of this world; no, in the case of those who identify themselves with the poor Christ and seek to establish solidarity with the dispossessed on this continent . . . Yes, in the case of those who wish to neutralize Christ's liberation by restricting or reducing it to a purely spiritual plane that has nothing to do with the concrete world of human beings; no, in the case of those who believe that Christ's salvation is so total and radical that nothing escapes it. For the latter, evangelization is liberative because it proclaims a total liberation in Christ that includes a transformation of concrete historical and political conditions on the one hand but also conducts that history above and beyond itself to a fulfilment that is not within the reach of human foresight or any human effort.[20]

When we do continue with our Storytelling, however, we shall need to apply a number of rigorous tests. *First,* our Stories must deal with history honestly and seriously and not try to escape it or smooth it over. They must confront the failure of Christianity to transform the world, not continually fantasize about its powers and achievements in either a missionary or development mode. *Second,* we should ask who tells any particular Story and why. We can never entirely avoid telling the Stories we like and which suit our purposes, but we can help each other – and the poor especially can help us – to be more aware of what we are doing than we often are. *Third,* our Stories must support those who seek to change history in the interests of the poor, not those who don't. A good Story can be very supportive indeed. If we can make reasonable sense of what we are doing it can be extremely energizing. It produces the very opposite of those crestfallen individuals who give up trying because, as they say: 'What's the point?' But that is the acid test. The Stories must not divert our efforts but enable us to give those efforts our wholehearted attention. They must steady our nerve, not cut the nerve of our historical endeavours. How many of our theologies do that?

Fourth (and the Story I have told about making a world with God allows for this), our Storytelling should take second place, or be subservient, to our practical endeavours to discover more effective ways to overcome poverty and injustice, to end famine and flood, and to make the world a habitat for us all. We certainly need to understand the world as well as we possibly can, but not in order to justify it, but in order to change it. In theological language that means that systematic and dogmatic theology will be the servants of social, pastoral and practical theology, and the validity of our teaching will be measured by the creativity of our practice. There will be a bias, in line with the Gospel's, in favour of theological endeavours which contribute to historical change in favour of the poorest.

So it will not be surprising if I now turn to ask questions about how our faith and theology can help us discern what to do about famine and flood, and how best to do it.

3

CHRISTIAN DOCTRINE AND DEVELOPMENT POLICY

My experience of famine in the Horn of Africa led me to re-examine my belief in a loving and powerful God. My experience of disastrous floods in Bangladesh led to doubts about the impact of Christianity and its claim to be redemptive and creative. Both of these experiences and the reflections they provoked strengthened my preference for theological work which promoted historical change in favour of the poor. In practice this could mean making disciplines like Christian social ethics and social theology the focus of our attention. For me it has often meant working hard as a Christian to build viable development policies and making sure that they were fully informed by Christian teaching. But the effort to relate Christian teaching or doctrine to development policy is not without its own difficulties. Three experiences, very different from famine and flood but still at the interface between Christianity and poverty, will I hope help to illustrate what they are. The first is my working experience with Christian Aid (1985–97), the aid and development agency of most of the British churches,[1] the second with the World Council of Churches and the third with an extensive study programme in twenty-one countries on 'Christianity, Poverty and Wealth in the 21st Century'.

1. Scepticism

Among the staff of Christian Aid there was widespread scepticism that Christian doctrine could make any significant contribution to development policies. There were several reasons for this. Here are six.

First, although there was a good deal of Christian idealism around, there was a tendency to be impatient with the institutional church and its teachings. The church was in decline. It was not very attractive or relevant. It was thought to have the wrong agenda, and it was not sufficiently interested in social and political issues. This impatience was despite the fact that churchgoers remained Christian Aid's most solid basis of support.

Second was the conviction (by no means confined to Christian Aid) that 'theology' was a largely theoretical, even other-worldly pursuit offering little, if anything, by way of practical results. It was not a suitable tool for the trade. There are strong echoes here of points made by the Southern theologians already referred to.[2] Much of the theology of Western Christianity lives in a self-contained, abstract world of its own. It is incapable of engaging with historical realities and may not wish to do so where the result could amount to a serious challenge to the status quo.

Third, there was an absence of in-house skills which could confidently deploy the methods of Christian social theology and social ethics to good effect.

Fourth, if anyone did want to take Christian doctrine seriously there was no solid and single tradition of Christian teaching to draw upon. Staff were confronted with the divisive history of Protestantism and, in the present, with a plurality of forty churches all sponsoring Christian Aid but with varying uncoordinated opinions, in stark contrast to the guidance available to, say, their colleagues in CAFOD, the Roman Catholic agency.

Fifth was the perception that once it was agreed on Christian grounds that abject poverty was unacceptable and should be overcome, the debates about how best to put an end to it were mainly of a more technical kind to which Christianity had no special wisdom to bring. It had nothing much to say about better methods of flood control in Bangladesh, or about 'sustainable livelihoods' which make sure that a family in Ethiopia has enough money to buy food when their own crops fail. Maybe issues like reconciliation and conflict resolution were more up its street but, as we have said,[3] they hardly become possibilities until the underlying conditions which generate war and poverty alike are changed; and working out how to change them takes us back into matters which are beyond the competence of Christianity. To take two other areas of debate, having protested against some appalling working conditions for children, in carpet factories, for example, Christians were no better placed than anyone else to suggest how to put an end to them without causing even greater hardship for the families involved by robbing them of a crucial source of income; and having insisted that refugees should be fed and sheltered as efficiently as possible, Christianity had little to add to the discussions about how you could do so without giving aid and comfort to troublemakers, among the Rwandans, for example, in the refugee camps in Zaire, or without discouraging the earliest possible return home to a degree of normality. If Christianity did have a contribution, it was not to the arguments that seemed to matter most.

Finally came the observation that if there were differences of opinion, ethical as well as technical, between development agencies, including government and UN agencies, the dividing line was rarely if ever between the Christians and the rest, or the cause of it their Christian beliefs. Christian teaching did not appear to be decisive, so therefore appeared to be relatively unimportant.

Having acknowledged this widespread scepticism, it would be misleading to suggest that Christianity did not play a significant role in the work of Christian Aid. It was and is, after all, an arm of the Christian churches and it needed to persuade those churches that what it did on their behalf and what it encouraged churchgoers to do themselves – often summed up at the time in the slogan: 'give, act and pray' – was in line with their Christian faith. As a result, educational and devotional materials would cite the biblical evidence in support of the struggle to end poverty, even if the contemporary struggle being advocated was a great deal less radical in its aims and methods than the biblical material might be heard to imply. Even statements of faith were espoused by Christian Aid in its mission statements. They were often of an interesting counter-cultural variety. They tended to cut against the grain of traditional expressions of faith, believing, for example, in political liberation much more than in personal salvation, and in 'life before death' rather than life after death.

Christianity of a certain kind then could inspire and motivate and offer an ethical ideal but, when it came to making development policy, its teachings (or doctrines) were not regarded as particularly useful, or productive, or relevant. The results of trying to put these teachings to work did not justify the effort involved. There was at least one notable exception to all of that, to which we will return.[4]

2. Disagreement

To turn to the second experience, in a good deal of my work with the WCC on development issues I experienced the same stand-off between Christian doctrine and development policy. I did a survey of the ecumenical response to poverty over fifty years from the 1940s. It revealed many statements by ecumenical conferences and consultations which had about them the aura of having been decisively informed by Christian teaching; but on careful examination they had not.[5] No doubt the yawning gap which became apparent had something to do with the widespread idea that practical Christian service was not the natural habitat of theology. The old ecumenical slogan: 'doctrine divides, service unites' was never actually true, but what credibility it had was based on the assumption that doctrinal issues were divisive and restricted largely to 'Faith and Order' issues, like baptism, ministry and eucharist, and that Christian service, including the service of the poor, need not be contaminated by them.

But if there was a stand-off between theology and the world of ecumenical development policy, in the broader realm of ecumenical social ethics there has been something of a set-to, and it was not over whether Christian doctrine should contribute to social policy-making but over how. The discussion is well documented[6] and I shall not describe it at length, but the starting point is a well-established and confident tradition of Christian social ethics. Whilst recognizing the importance and relevance of Christian doctrine for social policy-making, it accepted that there was no direct and simple way of applying it (though Karl Barth tried on occasions[7] and was criticized for doing so). The doctrine of the Trinity, 'social' or otherwise, does not immediately produce a social policy any more than a doctrine of the human person or the Fall produces an employment policy. There are a number of reasons for this, including the way in which doctrines are historically conditioned and variously interpreted, and the obvious point that more than one such doctrine will be relevant and they don't all point in the same direction. The most important reason, however, is that if Christian social policy is to be of any use it will have to come to terms with other accounts of reality besides the accounts which have been distilled over the years into Christian teaching. One is the account provided by careful empirical observation, that is, 'the facts'; others include the various accounts of how things work in the world provided by disciplines such as economics, the political and social sciences and technology. Christian policy-making does not have to be subservient to these 'facts' and disciplines. It is not required to take them simply at face value. It does not have to do as they apparently say without question; but it is required to take them seriously, enter into dialogue with them and give good reasons for accepting or rejecting their advice. Respect for these 'autonomous disciplines', as they are sometimes called, and for the 'experts' who practise them have therefore been prominent features of this approach to Christian policy-making; as have 'middle-axioms', which are attempts to provide guidelines for policy makers somewhere between generalizations and detailed policies out of a respectful encounter between Christian doctrine, the 'facts' of the matter, and these autonomous disciplines.

This well-established and confident tradition, running back to the Oxford Conference on Church Community and State of 1937 and to William Temple's short but classic book on *Christianity and Social Order*,[8] has been critical of how it has perceived the WCC and its associates going about the task of social policy-making in recent years within an ecumenical family now greatly enlarged, more varied and significantly influenced by the advent of the churches of the South and of the poor. Crudely stated, it has accused the WCC of being far too prejudiced (or ideological) and propagandist (for example, in its unduly negative attitude to the 'free-market' capitalist system, to globalization, to technology and environmental issues) and 'populist', if that is the right word, over relying on the views of 'the people' who are far less homogeneous than they are made out to be. The WCC is seen to have distrusted scientific method, rationality and expert opinion. It has failed to do justice to the diversity of situations confronting Christians and the opinions which they hold, and to foster a proper encounter between them. It has run the risk of 'passion without knowledge'. The 'traditionalists', if we can call them that, are in turn criticized for being élitist, robbing 'the people' of their voice and claiming to be 'objective' where they are equally biased and ideological in espousing, for example, capitalism and the relatively conservative notion of the Responsible Society.[9] In other words, they suffer from inescapable human characteristics to which, to be fair, they would admit.

3. Radical participation

For myself, I see no resolution of the argument except by way of what I would call 'radical participation'. The process of sounding out opinion will have the usual ecumenical concern for 'balance', with respect, for example, to gender, the generations and ethnicity but it will also accept the contribution that specialists and generalists, experts and lay people, academic disciplines and experience, theory and practice, passion and dispassionate analysis, can bring to policy-making. They will all be accompanied by their inevitable limitations, but it is ruling some of them out and not dealing seriously with variety and difference that will lead to the greatest inadequacies of policy-making.

Which brings me to the third area of my working experience, and to very recent difficulties and challenges to my faith. Christian development agencies like Christian Aid, mostly in Europe but related to the WCC, seized on the millennium not so much as an historical turning point as an opportunity to evaluate what they were doing and chart a fresh course for the future. They faced many challenges of their own and still do.[10] The New Labour British government, for example, had less time for NGOs (non-governmental organizations) as major partners in development. Their efficiency in emergency situations (which seem likely to increase in number) was being questioned. They remain locked into a North–South scenario which is increasingly outdated. The world they now have to operate in is vastly different from the world for which they were originally fashioned. Their independence is under threat as they rely more and more on government and European Union funding. Above all, perhaps, was the fear (unfounded) that the public would grow tired of supporting them if poverty in the world refused to go away and efforts to eradicate it seemed pointless. There were, and are, plenty of reasons for thinking again.

One of the upshots is a study programme, running from 1999 to at least 2001, which I was asked to direct on 'Christianity,

Poverty and Wealth in the 21st Century'. It will involve twenty-one countries round the world working to a similar brief. Each participant will ask, among other things, about the history of poverty in their own country or region and its causes, both internal and external, how it was perceived and what actions have been taken to redress it. They will be particularly interested in how Christians and their churches answer these questions in relation to their faith, but not exclusively so. They will go on to ask about the key factors relating to poverty which have to be reckoned with in the opening years of the new century (globalization, ethnicity and conflict are obvious candidates) and what kind of responses the churches in particular and their agencies should make and, more than that, what are the most promising responses, new models and approaches which are already proving to be creative and viable. In order to address these issues, the participants are expected to set up a wide-ranging process of fact-finding, consultation and debate within their own countries involving rich and poor, specialists and lay people, and to bring the fruits of their endeavours to a colloquium in India towards the end of the year 2000 and try to see together where to go from there.

One of the most important outcomes of a study like this should be a set of development policies for the future, and the method proposed for making them or arriving at them is an attempt at the kind of 'radical participation' to which I have already referred.

'Radical participation' is necessary, not only out of a sense of justice and respect for people, but because of our limited and sinful nature as human beings. That is not, of course, all there is to be said about us. 'Made in the image of God', we are all capable of being creative, which is why there is any point in the first place in encouraging everyone to contribute, and why it is foolish for any enterprise to be exclusive and deny itself insights and worthwhile contributions that are there, at least potentially, for the asking. Nevertheless, all of us contribute to any enterprise, in this case to development policy, from a limited point of view and one which can never entirely escape from the shadows of our own vested interests. Our knowledge is limited, our understanding is partial, our opinions are coloured by the accidents of our experience and by what we believe to be, rightly and often wrongly, to our advantage.

Our only hope of ameliorating the effects of these insufficiencies and distortions is by seeking to discern the way forward, including future development policy, together and not alone. Those who become our partners in this participative enterprise are of course as limited, partial and self-seeking as we are: the poor with their theology of liberation, for example, as much as the rich with their theology of the forgiveness of sins. They are, however, likely to be limited and partial at different points, and self-seeking in different ways, so that in encounters with one another there are opportunities to compare, criticize, correct and complement each other. The outcome is by no means perfect, but it is a more rounded discernment of policy and of ways forward than if that encounter had never taken place.

'Radical participation', of course, implies 'stakeholder participation' or participation by all the interested parties: women and men, young and old, poor and rich, the differently abled and disabled, white and black from South and North and East and West, and so on. But mindful of the disagreements within the ecumenical movement over how best to do Christian social ethics and therefore how best to arrive at sound development polices, radical participation can also be characterized by a series of 'both-ands'. Here are five: first, it includes both 'experts' and 'lay people', by which I mean not only lay and ordained but those well-versed in professional disciplines like economics or the social sciences and those without formal qualifications; second, both those who have learned what they know from academic study and those who have learned almost entirely from experience; third, both those with powerful positions in governments, corporations and institutions and the so-called 'uninfluential';

fourth, both the prophetic, clear-sighted campaigners and the experienced bureaucrats who can handle red tape and diplomacy; and fifth the 'both-and' of inter-faith dialogue.

This conviction that 'radical participation' of some such sort is essential if we are to arrive at anything like satisfactory development policies for the future is built into the design of the study programme on 'Christianity, Poverty and Wealth in the 21st Century' which I spoke about earlier in this section. It brings together the Christianity of the West and of the South and calls for a consultative process within each of the participating countries. It asks to hear from 'experts' and people's organizations, academics and practitioners. It requires an inter-disciplinary approach and is attracted to an action–reflection model which acknowledges the way in which the experiences and discoveries of practical obedience challenge, influence and inform our beliefs, just as our beliefs directly and indirectly influence what we do. Finally, this exercise in 'radical participation' , or this stage of it, culminates in a highly participative final colloquium.

4. Two unanswered questions

All this, however, leaves us begging a number of fairly large questions! I mention two.

First, participation, however 'radical' or thoroughgoing and comprehensive, can never be complete. Not every opinion can be represented, and not every opinion that is represented will be heard equally. Difficulties with language and the increasing dominance of English will make sure of that together with shortage of time and patience, the force of personality and in-built attitudes and prejudices. And the physical logistics of 'radical participation' are far from easy. Modern developments in interactive information technology with e-mail and web-sites and videos and 'virtual' conferences are an enormous help, but there is still much to learn about enabling many people from a wide variety of backgrounds to listen and talk productively to each other as, for example, yet another WCC Assembly (in Harare in 1998) underlined. The logistics of inclusive and extensive interaction between individuals and communities across the world, or of international networking, is a topic well worth talking about in its own right if we believe, as I do, that radical participation is the seed-bed of creativity and achieving it one of the fundamental tasks and understandings of ecumenism.[11] But however successful we are, any emerging social or development policy will still be open to the charge that to some extent it is partial and fails to take account of all the arguments. That, however, is no criticism. That is a fact of life. No policy is absolute. It should be taken seriously and put to the practical test, but it is never beyond question or improvement. No one suggests otherwise. 'Radical participation' does not produce perfect policies, and there is no guarantee that it will produce better policies (a single inspired genius, for example, may do just that ahead of all the painstaking colloquia the world can organize) but 'radical participation' has a better chance of producing wiser and better informed policies than procedures which are narrowly based.

A comment here about the so-called 'expert' who has come in for a deal of criticism, for example in the WCC-related debate about methodology in Christian social ethics and policy-making. Whatever suspicions may surround them, as being élitist, for example, and far less 'objective' and dispassionate than they like to think, experts cannot be dismissed too easily as peddling narrowly-based opinions. 'Expertise' implies knowing what you are talking about: you know about the history of your subject; you know about the range of opinions and where they come from; you know how certain principles and policies have been distilled over time out of long debate and growing evidence and practical experience; you can lay out the wide parameters of the subject. Experts are no substitute for 'radical participation', but they are in themselves, or should be, useful repositories of information and the products of a long and participative process.

Participation then, however radical and inclusive of experts and popular opinion, will not produce perfect development policies, but it has the potential to produce far better ones, at least for the time being.

The second big unanswered question is more difficult to handle. Assuming a highly participatory occasion such as a 'virtual' international networking conference or a colloquium on 'Christianity, Poverty and Wealth in the 21st Century', how should it proceed to discern a way forward and arrive at policies for the future? What are the rules of engagement when a whole range of opinions are brought together in this sort of encounter? On what basis does an emerging opinion establish itself and become accepted and regarded as 'valid'; or on what basis do you choose between two opinions when they don't happen to agree? 'Radical participation' may tell us who and what to bring together for policy-making, but it tells us very little about how to conduct our internal affairs – about an appropriate procedure or methodology – once we have done so.

I have three points to make. First, presumably there has to be some common ground at the outset for the project even to get started, and that common ground will exclude as well as include. There will need to be a shared aim, in this case to discover policies and practices that add up to an appropriate Christian response to poverty (and not all the Christian world is interested in that). There will also need to be a shared belief that radical participation is worthwhile and necessary: worthwhile because all of us have the gift of creativity and can make the kind of contribution which deserves a respectful hearing; and necessary because no contribution is entirely trustworthy, or beyond challenge and improvement, or likely to prove adequate on its own. This shared belief is clearly exclusive. It is the dividing line, for example, between the tolerant, non-absolutists who know we have to live with pluralism and relativism, and the absolutists who must be tolerated but who find it difficult to be tolerant in return.

Second, granted this common ground of shared aims and a shared eagerness to listen and learn, it seems quite hard to think of an agreed method of choosing between two or more opinions in the debates and arguments that will follow. What are the criteria by which policies will be judged and gain validity? Most appeals to independent arbitration may prove instructive, and in that sense necessary and worthwhile, but they are unlikely to be decisive unless, of course, everyone agrees for practical purposes to allow one of them sooner or later to have the final say. Six examples of a validity-test come to mind: first is the appeal to 'facts' whether scientific, economic, political or historical; second comes expert opinion grounded at its best in wide and detailed knowledge of the subject; third is experience most notably of what policies have succeeded or failed in the past, of what 'works' and what does not; fourth is the 'majority' view or what is sometimes referred to as the view of the 'people' or even of the poor masses who might be expected to know best what is best for them; fifth, and especially where we are relating Christian doctrine to development policy, comes the authority of the Bible and the church; and sixth is rationality, or instrumental reason, where one argument flows logically from another and policies are required to be coherent and free from inconsistencies.

All six ways of testing the validity of an emerging policy seem necessary and sensible enough to me, but each of them is open to challenge. 'Facts' and analyses are soon coloured by interpretations. 'Experts' disagree and are never entirely objective. Recently there has been a distrust of them over genetically modified (GM) foods and bio-technology, for example, in the Western world, and there is a long-standing distrust of economic and development experts in the poorer countries of the South. 'Experience' as a test could refer to scientific experiment or testing, or to the distilled accumulation of expertise over long periods of time and in many settings. But it could also refer to practical wisdom born out of a very restricted context, or to a highly subjective view of the matter in hand. Some experience will be far more weighty than others, though it is hard to challenge any of it if you cannot claim to have shared it. The 'popular' view, as a final court of appeal, can be just as divided as expert opinion. It can be based on wishful thinking, and it can tempt us into 'dumbing down' exercises which settle for the lowest common denominator. Biblical and church 'authorities' do not speak with one voice, certainly not in the Protestant world, and so perpetuate rather than resolve the problem of establishing who, if any, should have the final word. Finally, 'reason' and rationality and the assumption that they are possessed, understood and respected by all women and men have run into increasing trouble between the Enlightenment and the so-called 'post-Modernist' age. Common sense is not so common or sensible after all.

Let me add one or two further remarks about these six criteria I have listed as possibly validating an emerging development policy, or any other social policy for that matter. They are not, of course, totally discrete or mutually exclusive. 'Experts', for example, who ought by definition to know what they are talking about, could see their expertise as taking full account of all the criteria, including what vast numbers of 'lay people' may think. The 'action–reflection' model as a method of policy-making, to take another example, is sometimes criticized for abandoning rigorous study and debate and claiming to learn only from a somewhat haphazard and untested stream of experience whereas, properly understood, it sees careful analysis, rigorous thinking and practical allegiance to the insights gained as indispensable parts of the whole. Even Christian doctrine, as we shall underline again later, is far more the product of experience than the way many people handle it or, rather, refuse to handle it, would ever suggest. These six criteria then are not mutually exclusive, neither are they in my view to be dismissed out of hand. The fact that none of them qualifies as an absolutely reliable way of finally establishing the validity of an argument or policy, not even all of them put together, does not mean they are not useful and necessary tools in debate.

Even taken together, however, these six reference points will find it hard to rise above the fundamental differences of context, ideology, vested interest and faith which exist between those who are involved in exercises in 'radical participation' and which cannot easily be resolved or bridged, certainly not in the comparatively short timescale within which we have to construct our development policy. (One such fundamental difference may be all too obvious in the somewhat masculine, argumentative and conflictual picture I have inadvertently painted of intellectual problem solving?)

I come to a third point about the way to proceed towards valid conclusions within 'radical participation', which is to suggest that too much concern with methodology is probably a waste of time. Attempts to find criteria to settle arguments will only find themselves open to arguments in their turn. If by 'methodology' we mean 'radical participation', then it is certainly worth taking time to argue for it as I have tried to do. But if by 'methodology' is meant the rules of the game by which serious encounters between a wide variety of people and opinions are to proceed via various steps and mental processes towards making development policy, then I am no longer at all sure it is time well spent.

Within 'radical participation' a policy will not gain validity by way of correct methodological procedures. It will only be valid on a consensus basis where, out of serious encounters in which people have listened and learned and debated with each other, all have come to accept it as valid but for their own good reasons, some shared and some not. Common ground has eventually been mapped out and occupied, but the various parties have arrived at it by different routes. They have persuaded one another what their development policy and their responses to poverty should be. There is a shared conclusion, valid for all, but not necessarily by virtue of the same validation procedure or an appeal to a shared understanding of the Christian faith.

If this relative indifference to methodology is acceptable then, for example, the WCC debate I have referred to about methods in social theology and ethics could become a waste of time once it is established that many different contributions are needed if there is to be a valid outcome. Beyond that, the argument should not be about method but about substance and outcomes.

5. A personal methodology

Not wasting time on establishing an agreed methodology within radical participation in social ethics and social theology is not the same as saying that the participants, including myself, need not be concerned that their own conclusions, and the methods by which they arrive at them and defend them, stand up in their own eyes. I ought to be able to give an account of myself to myself and have at least self-respect for the policies I am prepared to adopt and advocate. But that is quite different from attempting to find a methodology that is universally acceptable. That is just not possible within our kind of world where 'relativism' and 'pluralism' are facts of life, even if they are interpreted facts!

Again, whilst I am against the search for a universal methodology, I am all in favour of each of us putting on the table the method that is acceptable to us and by which we try to make progress towards policies that are valid in our own eyes and expressive of our faith. Others, who may not accept the method for themselves, are nevertheless entitled to know the basis for our opinions and will be helped in their encounters with us if they understand why we think as we do. Likewise, we shall be helped by understanding as much as possible about their ways of thinking. For example, I have vivid memories of sitting with base Christian communities in South America and listening to them using Bible stories to analyse situations of conflict, such as the struggle for land, and how they should respond to them. Attractive as it was, I could not for one moment adopt their hermeneutical approach; and to a large extent the conclusions they drew from it seemed to me to be arbitrary. The whole conversation, however, was illuminating. It increased my understanding and helped in establishing common ground between us.

I have mentioned the dreaded word 'relativism'. Sitting light to methodological questions within 'radical participation', as I am proposing to do, does not I believe sink us into the kind of relativism which is often accused of regarding all opinions as equally valid with nothing to choose between them, or the kind which is so acutely aware of our differences that it questions whether the idea of a common humanity seeking common ground means anything at all. That is certainly not how I feel about it.

Absolute authorities and final courts of appeal may be hard to find these days, but there are many insights and criteria which command widespread respect. Take as an example the growing respect for universal human rights. In a world where nothing is final, not everything is equally unstable. Or again, if the nature of 'reason' and what reason readily appreciates is not as obvious as it was, we still appear to know how to take one another seriously in debates as, if you like, reasonable people and we find talking across cultural divides well worthwhile. And arguments and efforts to get agreement on matters like our response to poverty are not experienced by this pluralist and relativist as intellectual ping-pong games where anything goes. There is a serious, even morally serious, drive on many sides towards consensus and, as a Christian, I have enough confidence in our moral and creative capacities as human beings to believe that, not perfectly or finally or always, but often enough, a useful measure of consensus can be achieved.

I have referred to three areas of my own working experience: with Christian Aid, within the ecumenical family of the WCC, and organizing a study programme on 'Christianity, Poverty and Wealth in the 21st Century'. In each of them I have been concerned with the engagement between Christian doctrine and development policy and how the one informs the other, and each has presented difficulties and challenges for what I regard as my working faith. When it comes to method in Christian social theology and social ethics I have explained my attraction to 'radical participation', my doubts about spending time on methodological questions within that context, but my acceptance nevertheless of the need for me to be able to explain to others and justify to myself how I personally go about forming my own opinions and, since, of course, I want to do that in as participatory a way as possible, how I go about contributing to serious encounters in a highly pluralist church and world.

I want therefore, in the final part of this chapter, to list a number of methodological procedures and points that I try to observe in arriving at development policies, especially when trying to ensure that they are informed by Christian doctrine or teaching. I have ten brief points to make.

1. When talking about Christian doctrine or teaching informing development policy, I mean Christian doctrine or teaching as I understand it and accept it at the moment. Although a great deal of Christian teaching endures, indeed often clothes itself in permanence (in the historic creeds, for example), sometimes for good reasons because it proves to be valuable and sometimes for not so good reasons, it nevertheless changes. One source of change is the very process we are now engaged in of 'confronting' our beliefs with the realities of our lives including the harsh reality of poverty, where Christian teaching will often find itself severely challenged. Our discussion of theodicy and the idea that God is both loving and powerful in the face of famine and the normality of suffering, and our discussion of Christianity's claim to be redemptive in the face of disastrous floods and the 'unstable stable state' of history, are two examples of that. Not only does Christian teaching change, I find myself agreeing with parts of what it says to me but not with everything. If I am wise I shall not take this as the surest guide to what is true and I shall try to be well informed about the history of Christian ideas and the different strands of them in the contemporary Christian community. I shall try to be aware of why I like what I like and take seriously those elements of Christian teaching that I prefer to

reject. But at the end of the day I can only inform my development policy and practice with the Christian teaching that I
receive and understand and can say 'Yes' to now.

2. Christian teaching can support our social action in many
ways. It can motivate us, console us, inspire and encourage us.
Our interest at the moment, however, is in the contribution it
can make to the substance or content of development policy,
informing what we do once we are motivated and encouraged to
do it; and here I am attracted to the action–reflection model or
what is sometimes referred to as the pastoral cycle. It is not
unrelated to the rule of thumb (of liberation and other, older
theologies): 'see, judge, act'. The action–reflection model involves rigorous intellectual disciplines, to which we shall come,
but it also requires me to put into practice the policies I construct
not only as a way of being faithful to them – of doing 'the truth' –
but as a way of learning. By so doing I shall expect to achieve
greater insight which will force me to think again and move on to
further rigorous intellectual work. The long-running argument
about whether we learn the truth from revelation or from reason
or from experience is, of course, a false one. We can say we learn
from all three. We can also say there is nothing other than
experience, which is often 'revealing', to learn from. But the
argument about the relative importance of theory and practice
(which has popped its head up, for example, in the argument
about social ethics within the WCC family) is not a false one.
Theory, and doctrines are theories, has an important part to play.
It usefully organizes our experience of the world within and
about us into frameworks of understanding that can be carried
from one place to another. Theories and doctrines are indispensable summaries and packages of knowledge and understanding
against which to test our immediate experience. But all too often
doctrine becomes doctrinaire, dictating to reality rather than
making sense of it. It becomes destructive, out of touch and
unhelpful, because it has not been kept close enough to the
ground from whence, as a matter of fact, it came since it was no

more than distilled experience in the first place. And that is not
only true of Christian doctrines and theories. The policies of
International Financial Institutions like the World Bank and the
International Monetary Fund would frequently have been more
helpful to poor people and countries if its economists, who can
sometimes sound like fundamentalist preachers, spent less time
in their ivory towers and had more practical involvement in
development programmes. Their doctrinaire attitudes over debt
and structural adjustment are only now being broken down.
So theory and practice, rigorous thinking and practical action
and learning, must all go together in the action–reflection model:
one of the arguments, as we have said, in favour of 'radical
participation'.

3. When it comes to 'rigorous thinking' and 'intellectual discipline' – to those moments in the midst of practice when for one
reason or another we are forced to stop and think again or to
those moments when we deliberately stand back and collect our
thoughts – there are for me three basic questions we always need
to ask. The first is 'analytic'. What precisely is the situation we are
dealing with? What, for example, in a study on 'Christianity,
Poverty and Wealth in the 21st Century' is the nature of so-called
'poverty'? What are its characteristics? What is the extent of it?
What are the causes? Who are the players? How is poverty
different now from in the past, including the biblical past? In a
mixture of so-called fact and interpretation we have to describe
as accurately as we can the phenomenon we are dealing with or
we shall not deal with it well. No one will be helped by people
who completely misread or misunderstand what is going on or
don't even wait to check it out. That was largely my concern
when faced with too much talk of repentance and reconciliation
after the genocide in Rwanda.[12] The second question is about
'goals'. Given our analysis of where we are, where is it we want to
be? What, in a study on 'Christianity, Poverty and Wealth in the
21st Century' is the reversal or opposite of the poverty we set out
to overcome? What changes do we wish to bring about in our

social and economic life? What are our objectives? The third question is about 'process', or ways and means. How do we get from where we are to where we want to be, or at least further along the road and in the right direction? What is possible and what is not? What actions are likely to hinder progress and what are most likely to help? Incidentally, I hope it is not hard to see how these three questions can live happily with a 'Story' about redeeming the times or better still about creating a world for the very first time where we need to understand the nature of the raw material we have to work with (analysis), imagine a suitable home for all of us to enjoy (goals), and learn how to make or create it (process).

4. After these three big questions comes the hard work of searching for the answers, or shall we say some relevant responses to them. Here we either need the confidence which assumes that Christian teaching has some of those answers, or we forget about this whole enterprise of policy-making as Christians and understand our faith as something which may comfort and support us in our endeavours but which cannot really add to them anything of substance. I choose the road of confidence not least because of my understanding of doctrine as basically the distillation of our experience in the first place. So, to take the first question, Christian teaching does, I believe, engage with our attempts to analyse and describe our human condition, including the condition of poverty and the world we live in, so that we respond to it appropriately. The Christian doctrines of Creation, the Fall and of Human Nature are evidence of that, though what they teach us is not, of course, universally agreed. For example, there are those these days, encouraged by mounting environmental disaster, who regard the natural world as having an untouchable integrity, whilst others believe it needs the constant attention of a sympathetic but creative gardener. Some will see sinful human nature mainly as perversity whilst others, including myself, regard it as insecurity. To take the second question, Christian teaching does, I believe, make proposals about the goals that are worth striving

for, and has prototypes for worlds that are preferable to this world. Again its teaching about human persons and their communities, the high value it gives to love and justice, and its visions of the Kingdom are evidence of that. So are movements like Christian Socialism honouring the equality of all women and men, and contemporary ecumenical slogans like: 'Justice, Peace and the Integrity of Creation'. And when we come to consider the 'process' or ways and means, Christian teaching is, I believe, full of suggestions about how we are to move from where we are to where we want to be, preventing the worst and promoting the better. All its redemptive theories or doctrines of atonement are evidence of that, even though they have been far too narrowly interpreted in Christian history as explanations of the work of Christ and how Christ has saved us from our sins.[13]

Christian doctrine is 'porous', useful and useable. It grew up out of attempts to answer our questions and it will go on doing so; and it can be unpacked and unravelled to deliver up the wisdom it has gathered over the years.

5. Christian doctrine is a very generalized way of packaging Christian insights that can inform our policy-making. Just as useful, if not more so, are traditions of Christian teaching on particular subjects. When it comes to lending and borrowing in development, for example, whether at the level of public international debt or private investment or micro-credit schemes, much has already been said on 'usury'. We shall want to make good use of it and not reinvent the wheel. But we shall not be uncritical, and one way of unpacking it and asking questions and in so doing informing our own thinking is to 'deconstruct' it and see out of what analysis and ideas about goals and ways and means of achieving them it arose. In *Life After Debt*[14] Michael Northcott, concerned about the supremacy of economic interests on the global scene, discusses what he calls 'good governance'. The discussion is heavily dependent on Christian teaching about the state and on Oliver O'Donovan's more recent writing on political theology.[15] His conclusions, however, can be decon-

structed (which is not the same, of course, as destroying them), not only as a way of examining and reflecting on them more closely, but as a way of drawing on them for our own policy-making. What Northcott has to say includes an analysis which suggests that the power to govern is being taken away from political institutions into the hands of economic ones; it includes a discussion of the goals to be achieved, in this case fairer trading systems which operate for the good of all without damaging the environment; and it includes proposals as to how this is to be achieved, in other words the process, especially by way of international institutions answerable to a body of international law which promotes the common good rather than sectional interests. His discussion illustrates how more specific teaching as well as doctrine relates to and revolves round the three fundamental questions about 'analysis', 'goals' and 'process'.

6. I do not believe that in principle it is at all difficult to take these Christian responses to the three fundamental questions and incorporate them into the inter-disciplinary work which most of us agree is essential for constructing adequate social policies, including development policies; and that is because all the other disciplines address them as well. Take any of them: economics or social science or development itself, for example, or even a highly technical discipline like agriculture, and we find them behaving just like theology. They will be busy analysing an unworkable economy or a situation of conflict or a disastrous crop failure or flood, wanting to find out exactly what is going on. They will be setting goals like the social market or power-sharing in Northern Ireland or a green revolution or an inclusive society; and they will be looking for economic or political measures and procedures or agricultural techniques that are likely to move things forward. All the disciplines then involved in this inter-disciplinary enterprise address the same three questions and are to that extent comparable and compatible and have strong points of contact between them.

7. The fact that all disciplines have much in common, not least

the basic questions they address, does not mean that they will all deserve or require equal attention on every occasion of rigorous reflection or practice. I can think of two reasons why. On any particular occasion the answers of some disciplines will be more relevant than others, seed science, for example, more than parables of the sower, and the instinct of aid and development workers in Christian Aid that theology would not be all that helpful could often therefore be right, especially when the issues are highly technical. I do not believe, however, that Christian teaching is ever entirely irrelevant. Or again, some disciplines may demand less work of us at times in deciding what they have to say in response to the questions of the moment, since by nature they are more stable and conservative or have, for the time being, well-established and generally accepted views. Christian doctrine tends to be stable and conservative. It changes, as we have said, not least in the light of our experience and context. But it does not change all that much or all that often and 'paradigm-shifts' in any discipline are not everyday occurrences. So the teaching of a particular discipline, including Christian teaching, may remain equally relevant but sometimes preoccupy us less.

8. Quite often the contribution of Christian doctrine is reduced to a concern with upholding moral values such as justice and equality. Of course there are Christian values to be upheld, not least when we consider the goals we intend to pursue and how we should deal with people when we pursue them. There is also a hierarchy of values to be upheld: human happines, for example, above economic growth. But Christian teaching has a far wider curriculum than that and has a lot to say about many other topics besides what may be the right thing to do. It can hold analytical conversations about the nature of things. It can hold 'strategic' conversations about how best to go about things. Much of its teaching is not in the imperative mood at all, but in the indicative mood. It talks about what 'is' the case as well as what 'ought to be' the case about the world and ourselves and how it all works and how it can be transformed. It is descriptive

as well as evaluative. Christian teaching does not come into play over only a limited part of the policy-making agenda, but across the whole of it. It does not only respond to some of the questions, but to all three of them.

9. When it comes to making a decision about what our answers will be, I do not see that there is some intellectual procedure whereby the contributions of many varied disciplines, including theology, can be properly related to each other or combined in order to produce something like an intellectually automated answer, rather like putting the correct ingredients into a bread-making machine and producing a loaf. We shall, of course, compare them and think carefully about the points at which they contradict one another or appear to be incompatible. And we shall test the validity of our emerging conclusions as best we can against the expert opinions we respect. And they will be tested later for their fruitfulness in the hard world of practical obedience. But at this particular moment of reflection, having considered and absorbed the contributions of all the disciplines, including Christian doctrine, we are left to a large extent to take our courage in both hands and quite literally 'make up' our own minds. We have to exercise our creativity by making a judgment of our own. That judgment, however, will be better informed and made out of a richer stock of insights and ideas and possibilities than if we had failed to adopt an inter-disciplinary approach. The process has, perhaps, more to do with formation than with formulas. Gathering and pondering the insights of many teachers will form and transform the minds which in the end have to be left to draw their own conclusions.

10. Conclusions having been drawn, there is one further step in the methodology which I as a Christian would try to follow in making development or any other social policy. It is a kind of checking procedure. Having made up our minds, we can then ask whether the judgment we have made is in harmony with or coherent with our understanding of Christian doctrine and teaching, whether set out systematically or in narrative form as

the Story we tell. It is not a matter of asking whether a policy fully embodies or reflects Christian teaching. That will not always be possible, because of all the other considerations which have to be taken into account and the compromises and trade-offs that have to be made. Neither is it a matter of ensuring that the Christian contribution is always explicit or distinctive and the outcome always different from everybody else's. That is certainly not the case if you look at the broad consensus between aid and development agencies, Christian or otherwise, and even between agencies and governments over development policies today, and it is not necessarily any the worse or less 'Christian' for that. Indeed, I would argue at times that a less blatantly Christian policy could well be more productive and therefore more Christian. It is, however, important to ask how far any policy and Christian teaching can live with each other. If not at all then rigorous thinking requires us at the very least to think again. In the next chapter I want to look at some of that teaching – about atonement – especially in relation to our third question about how we should go about making the world we believe God has in mind for us.

We have already referred to one explicit attempt to bring Christian doctrine to bear on development policy, in particular on the issues of debt, trade and governance, and it reflects something of the interdisciplinary approach I have described.[16] Other issues include structural adjustment policies, conflict resolution, co-operatives, sustainable livelihoods, the 2015 UN targets for poverty reduction, a global social market, disasters and emergencies, the environment and communities of counter-culture and resistance. In all of these Christian doctrine can contribute to a richer stock of responses to the basic questions of analysis, goal-setting, and process as well as asking whether such policies, once constructed though not necessarily distinctively Christian, are coherent with its own understanding of human and divine reality.

Here then is the method I personally would adopt, and here is the method I would describe as my own in a situation of 'radical participation', not to promote it or prescribe it as universally valid, but in order to increase understanding of why I argue and debate with others as I do. In doing so I shall not, of course, be able to hide from them completely the other reasons (some would say the 'real' reasons) why I argue and debate with them as I do. They include my vested interests, my formation within a Western Christian tradition which arouses deep suspicions in the poor, and a social and historical context which can scarcely now be shed; and they are just as powerful in determining policy and practice as any of the self-conscious methods which I care to adopt. Hence our need of one another!

4

LEARNING HOW TO MAKE

1. A balance of power

Amidst widespread scepticism within Christian Aid, there was one area of Christian teaching which was generally regarded as useful when it came to development policy-making. It was even incorporated as the central motif of its 'mission statement' in the 1980s called *To Strengthen the Poor*. I associate it mainly with Reinhold Niebuhr and his classic writings about moral man and immoral society.[1] His clear-eyed Christian realism did not underestimate our human capacity for self-transcending love and generosity. But that capacity could never be wholly relied upon, even less so when we act as social groups rather than individuals; and it was not the only factor to be reckoned with. A Christian analysis of human nature revealed a darker side to it which, out of a deep-seated insecurity far more than sheer perversity, leads us to protect ourselves and defend what we perceive to be our own self-interests against the interests of others. What power we have as nations or classes or organized capital or labour we shall use for these purposes, and the weaker we are the more vulnerable we shall be to policies that benefit only someone else.

The kind of strategy hinted at in the Magnificat (Luke 1.46–55) and informing many a revolution is no solution. To remove the mighty from their thrones and exalt the humble and meek and those of low degree is only to offer another social group the opportunity to behave like the one before, once power is in their hands. One oppressor with his egocentric behaviour is simply replaced by the next. History proves that their generosity is not to be relied upon. Given that an imbalance of power is the fundamental occasion of injustice and therefore of poverty, what is required is not a change of power but a better balance of power and more checks and balances within power structures so that the rulers of this world cannot lord it over others without let or hindrance.

Christian teaching, therefore, together with other disciplines which help us to understand how human societies work, produces a useful 'rule of thumb' for policy-making: will it or will it not promote a balance of power? It was this teaching that inspired Christian support for the trade union movement. The same teaching inspired the controversial programme to combat racism adopted by the WCC in 1969. If there was ever to be justice for black people in Southern Africa, their liberation movements, including their liberation armies, had to be supplied with resources more equal to those of the powerful vested interests (mainly white) ranged against them. The same teaching led to Niebuhr's support for democracy, believing that the creative and generous side to human nature makes democracy possible and the darker side makes it necessary. A more contemporary version of that, especially where so-called democracies are all too easily high-jacked by the rich and the powerful, is a commitment to strengthen civil society so that ordinary people have their say in decision-making. This rule of thumb also applies in the economic sphere where the debate has shifted since the liberation movements and armies of Africa and Central America came to an end. The root of economic injustice is an imbalance of economic power where capital, for example, can move freely across the world to speculate and make money, but labour cannot. Multinationals can often overrule the nation state. The 'free-market' spells opportunity to the powerful, but is a constant threat to smaller producers. Poor countries are exploited, whilst rich ones are protected. Arguments about fair trade policies, democratizing International Financial Institutions like the World Trade Organization, internalized economies which are less dependant on the global market, alliances of nations in economic communities, global governance to control the global economy, are all to do with a better balance of power where the 'mighty' and those of 'low degree' don't change places but are more evenly matched.

Insuring, however, that any policy for development contributes to a better balance of power is an exercise in preventing the worst rather than achieving the best. That does not make it unimportant and on many occasions we would do well to get even that far, but it is not enough.

I want now to describe four more characteristics or criteria of the struggle to replace poverty and injustice with a fairer world. I suppose I have come to regard them as essential. They are all positive in tone and in terms of my three questions about 'analysis', 'goals' and 'process' they relate to the third: 'process'. They all have to do with the crucial question about how we actually behave in ways that are constructive rather than destructive or merely preventative, and how we successfully move from where we are towards where, with the goal of God's Kingdom on our horizons, we want to be. They could be regarded as the fruits of a learning process involving action and reflection: 'learning how to make'. They could also be regarded as a kind of credal statement of what I and I hope some others believe are marks of creativity. I will introduce them by way of four stories from my own experience. They are for me paradigm cases of so much else. I will then discuss how these four marks are related to Christian faith.

2. Four marks of creativity

1. Some years before the civil war in Somalia (1992), with its almost total breakdown of law and order and the disastrous intervention of the US, I travelled for two days to the North-East of the country over deeply rutted roads and tracks which were

often better avoided than used. The desert sand frequently offered a smoother surface! Even in those days travelling was not safe. An armed guard accompanied us as protection from war-lords who might well commandeer our vehicle as they had com-mandeered others. Our destination was a nomadic community in what we came to call 'camel country'. Once there we would sit and sleep on camel skins, eat camel's meat and drink camel's milk. The herds of cattle, camels and goats were endlessly moved from place to place in the search for water. The herdsman would be the father of several families with wives and children in the different watering-places. His mother, the matriarch of this extended family, would often accompany him as a kind of travelling adult education unit, teaching the younger women the traditional skills of homemaking. The land, unlike its people, seemed arid and inhospitable. To me it was not only a very different country, it was an entirely different age, little affected by anything I regarded as 'modern'.

All the more astonishing, therefore, to be taken to see banks of solar panels gleaming in the desert sun. Row upon row of photo-electric cells were absorbing the rays of the sun and converting its energy into electricity which in turn drove the pumps which drew up the water from deep below the surface. It poured out into huge tanks like great round swimming pools. From there the water was piped in at least three directions: to standing pipes and taps where women and children collected it for drinking and washing; to troughs where camels and other animals waited their turn to drink; and to gardens where the community was growing tomatoes and green vegetables to supplement their diet. I visited at least half a dozen of these high-tech oases.

To find this technology within the setting of such an ancient nomadic culture was itself surprising (though I had to remind myself that the internal warfare which constantly scarred Somalia was also high-tech). But there was an equally impressive surprise to come. The solar panels were not without their problems, but they had not gone the way of some other forms of Western technology misguidedly exported by developers for the benefit of the so-called Third World. Other parts of the Horn of Africa (and our visit to Somalia took us literally on to the 'Horn' itself) I had visited were littered with tractors. Having done the fragile topsoil more harm than good, they now stood idle because there was no-one with the know-how or the parts to repair them. The solar panels and water pumps in 'camel country', however, were working perfectly well, the main reason being that the community had been involved at every turn. It was a Somali who had promoted the idea in the first place. It was the herdsmen and their families who had agreed that one of their greatest needs was for reliable supplies of water, clean enough for their families to drink. It was the local elders who, having consulted their people, had decided where the wells should be dug and the pumps and solar panels installed. It was these Somali nomads who had learned how to install the equipment and how to maintain the machinery and keep the panels spotlessly clean and turned towards the sun. It was the people's council which controlled the use of the water. It was an exercise in thoroughgoing participation and there seemed to me to be a direct connection between that and the kind of creativity that makes a new world: one small part of this desert had blossomed like a rose and become the sustainer of life.

One of the sadder experiences of that visit to Somalia was to go through village after village where motorized water pumps had been installed some years before but now stood neglected. We were told that they were the work of outside engineers on behalf of the government. The villagers had never been involved.

Participation is practised widely in development circles. Certainly much lipservice is paid to it, whether local programmes from education to health care are being planned, or democracy and civil society are being promoted at the national level. It inspires what is sometimes referred to as the 'non-operational' approach which refuses to do things for people or over their heads but at the very least works with them and at best enables them to do what they are perfectly capable of doing for themselves. It guards against the assumption that outsiders know best, even if an outsider's perspective can be useful. It accepts that people, whether rich or poor, are as wise as anyone about what is best for them and how to bring it about. Participation respects their ability and assumes that everyone has a contribution to make. Examples of it are too numerous to mention. Its importance has been taken up into more recent debates about 'inclusion'.

There are several reasons why participation has a positive or, we might say, creative effect. For one thing, we are likely to be far more responsible when we are involved and far more interested in what we own and what we want. Participation motivates. For another, it breeds confidence and self-respect. For another, if there is learning to be done, being involved is a good way to learn. For yet another, drawing on all the talents rather than assuming that very few exist or, for example, that a nomadic community could never install and maintain a solar pump, is to maximize the wealth we share between us.[2]

2. A second mark of creativity was typified for me by one of several visits to Brazil. Brazil is one of the world's leading economies, but its population includes a high percentage of very poor people. Vast areas of land are owned by comparatively few wealthy landowners. Millions of the poor are landless. According to Brazilian law, if land is left uncultivated the poor have the right to possess it. But that is easier said than done in a vast country where national state law is one thing and local and regional practice another.

The movement of the landless in Brazil is highly participatory. It is organized by landless people themselves and its members are intimately involved in its activities. It is also highly confrontational. The first of my three days – and nights – was spent with a community that had literally moved only that morning on to land they believed was theirs. I slept, or tried to sleep, in an upstairs room of a disused and dilapidated farmhouse. The farmland had lain fallow for years. Surrounding the house were fragile booths or shelters hastily erected to give some protection to women and children against the night air. They were made of little more than wooden poles and plastic sheets. The road to the farm was guarded. We ourselves were challenged on arrival. And the camp, including the upstairs room I shared with twenty others, was patrolled by what I later realized were armed watchmen. These desperate people expected the local militia to arrive at any moment. Whatever the law, powerful landowners would see to it that they were forcibly removed. Injury and death could not be ruled out. A sense of danger, however, was not the only emotion. There were stirring speeches to stiffen everyone's morale. There were songs of celebration. There were dominoes to play and smokey pipes to enjoy. We didn't get much sleep!

I spent a second day with another community which had been occupying land for seven or eight months. They had been forcibly removed as expected more than once. Not all had survived the ordeal, but most had returned. Gradually they had strengthened their foothold. The plastic shelters had been replaced by wooden shacks. Plots of land had been cultivated. Temporary schools had been opened for the children. Emissaries had been sent to state departments to make a case for transferring the land to the community. It was nearly Christmas and it was confidently expected that these landless people would be granted the deeds to their land by the turn of the year.

3. The third community I visited had more or less won their battle. The valley and the shallow hills on either side were theirs. The school and the houses were now more permanent, made of bricks with white painted walls and red tiled roofs. In one area we saw a chicken farm with a somewhat bored teenager left to take her turn to feed and water the birds in a vast free-range but crowded hen-house. A third was being built nearby. In another part of the valley we saw herds of milking cows and in another fields of grain and vegetables. There was plenty of food to eat and surplus produce for the markets. When I was shown what they called their 'cathedral', a modest three-sided shelter with a simple

altar, a crucifix, a picture of the 'good shepherd' with a bleeding heart and another of the Virgin Mary, it seemed almost natural to thank God that these exiles had returned home safely to possess their 'Promised Land'.

The confrontation typified for me by this 'paradigm case' is not quite the same as the confrontation which will eventually occur wherever vested interests are threatened. It is more pro-active than that. It deliberately takes the offensive. It asks for trouble where otherwise there might have been peace and quiet. The *Kairos Document* from South Africa[3] helps us to define what is meant. It outlined three 'theologies' or attitudes to the state, which was then the apartheid state or regime. The first acquiesces to injustice on the pretext that Paul's letter to the Romans, chapter 13, teaches Christians to be obedient to the ruling powers which are appointed by God. The second, 'Church Theology', recommends the path of reconciliation. It makes a kind of treaty with injustice. It accommodates or relates to it in a more or less amicable way. It ameliorates the affects of injustice, but does not root it out. The third theology is confrontational. It refuses to be silent or inactive in the face of evil. It is prophetic theology. It refuses to evade or overlook the issue. There may be tactical reasons at times for avoiding a head-on collision, but what is wrong is always tackled. There is no turning a blind eye. There is no living in the world, to quote I think Paul Tillich, 'as if' poverty and racism and landlessness and injustice do not exist. They have to be confronted. Creativity here is the opposite to a quiet life.

In the case of the landless of Brazil and many another libera-tion movement, confrontation has often involved taking up arms. That is not, however, necessarily the case. Indeed, many have argued[4] that violence only breeds violence and that non-violent confrontation is in the end just as effective and more creative. Non-violence is argued for at length by Walter Wink.[5] It was practised, for example, by Archbishop Romero in El Salvador when he read out publicly day after day in defiance of the military regime the names of the tortured and the disappeared; and it was practised by vast numbers of church leaders and members in South Africa when anti-apartheid demonstrators stood eye-ball to eye-ball with the security police.

Confrontation sounds like a negative rather than a creative activity, but it turns the spotlight on injustice. It exposes evil for what it is and provokes it into further exposure. It is forced into justifying itself and defending itself, thereby revealing the weakness of its own case. Challenged and weakened, it is put on the run. Thrown into doubt and disarray rather than allowed to go unchallenged, and with nothing convincing to say for itself, its morale is eroded and it is eventually overcome.

Solidarity, as a third mark of creativity, is part of the everyday jargon of the struggle against poverty. Two experiences gave it, for me, an added dimension. Senegal surrounds the Gambia in West Africa. Like Gambia, its people are extremely poor, especially in the rural areas. I spent a week travelling round the south of Senegal with a group of young men and women. They had all been to university and with their degrees had a good chance of escaping the poverty trap. Instead they had decided to go back to their villages and work with their own people. On visits to South Africa in some of the darkest days of the apartheid regime I met countless 'heroes and heroines of the faith' as I called them (thinking of Hebrews 11), doing their level best to stand by those in exile or in or out of prison or in hiding or in danger, and the families who suffered with them. Most of these heroes and heroines were black. Some were white. Perhaps the best known was Beyers Naude. I met him in his house. At the time he was a banned person and had been so for a number of years. As we talked, his wife, according to his banning order, was supposed to leave the room. He could not keep company with more than one person at a time. The house was bugged. Beyers Naude was a minister of the white Dutch Reformed Church. He was a member of the Brudebund. He belonged to social and religious circles which could be described as bastions of apartheid. He had cut his ties with all of them to stand instead with their victims who had come to regard him as one of their greatest friends and a most revered colleague and confidant.

Solidarity has a great deal to do with the poor and oppressed standing together. In these two cases and for me paradigmatically in the case of Beyers Naude, it was more. The Senegalese graduates and the villagers were on different sides. Beyers Naude and the blacks of South Africa were on different sides. Opportunity on one side; unremitting poverty on the other. Status and privilege on one side; relentless hounding by frightened and racist oppressors on the other. Solidarity here is not a matter of standing by everyone else on your side. It means changing sides and in a thoroughgoing way. It is not merely sympathy for the other side or for another point of view expressed from a safe distance. And it is not a selective form of approval which supports what it likes and distances itself from the rest. Solidarity of this sort 'takes sides' – the other side to where you might be expected to be – with all the biased strength that that phrase implies. Of course you may be critical of what is said and done by what is now 'your side', but that is never a reason to waiver from your underlying commitment to its cause. Solidarity involves staying with people through thick and thin, through their good and evil, to the extent that their reputation becomes yours and you suffer with them the consequences of what they do. What happens to them will happen to you. This is not the cool objectivity of a third party content to see the pros and cons of both sides and ensure fair play. The poor and oppressed will, at one level, never be morally superior to the wealthy and oppressive, but their poverty and oppression is beyond any defence. Solidarity becomes a kind of partisanship, almost a form of prejudice, in their favour.

If we ask why being partisan in this way can be creative, it clearly contributes to a shift in the balance of strength. It brings with it fresh skills and experience and wider perspectives, all of which are welcome, without forgetting that it will also be a learning experience for the partisans themselves: the talents are never on one side only. But just as important, if not more so, may be the

psychological and pastoral fruits of solidarity. To find the unexpected on your side can begin to qualify the sense of being
alone and abandoned, facing implacable opposition, the bearers
of a lost cause. To know that those you perceived of only as 'the
others', or 'the opposition', or as those who not being for you are
against you, are with you and are prepared to share your identify,
can bring with it the kind of reassurance and encouragement that
breed fresh energy and faith in your cause.

4. A fourth mark of creativity is typified for me by the story of
Chico Mendes. I met him only once, over five days in 1988. For a
short time he became a hero of the international environmental-
ist or green movement. I knew him as the leader of the rubber
tappers. They lived, and what is left of them still do, in the forests
of the Amazon. Each of them has an agreed pathway through the
trees and thickets which they walk twice a day. In the morning
they make an incision in the bark of each rubber tree in their care
and leave the sap or latex to bleed out and run down and be
caught in a surprisingly large husk, now empty of Brazil nuts.
Later in the day they return to collect the latex, ready to take it
to market. Some of the rubber tappers are quite young. They
told me that the nearby towns did not attract them and that
they enjoyed their way of life. It was, however, under threat.
Great swathes of the forest were being opened up to so-called
'developers'. They were clearing roads, bringing in machinery,
cutting down the trees, especially the hardwoods, for export and
turning the land over for cattle feeding, only to find that in a few
years time it no longer produced enough grass to feed the cattle
and the trees refused to grow again. A luxuriant forest was turning to desert. The developers made money for themselves and
boosted the country's export earnings, so helping to pay off its
debts, but they ruined the environment and the livelihoods of the
rubber tappers.

Chico Mendes, a Catholic layman, organized the rubber
tappers into a workers' organization. They confronted the
developers and the government head on. By way of protest they

sat down in front of the huge cutting and clearing machines to halt their progress. They took the matter to court and, when I was there, had already won a significant victory. Parts of the forest were to be protected. Reservations would be created within which the rubber tappers could continue their way of life, to which incidentally they had come generations ago as refugees from the poverty of the cities.

Organized rubber tappers were, however, a threat to the vested interests of landowners who could earn far more by destroying the forest than by preserving it. Chico Mendes pointed out to me more than once during my visit the landowners henchmen, as they drove their cars about or walked the streets of the town brandishing their guns. They had about them an air of menace.

On the last evening of our visit we had supper with Chico Mendes, his wife and their two children, in the kitchen of their small wooden house. Some of the animals could be seen underneath through the slats of the floor. Within a month after we left Chico Mendes had been killed by the gunmen in the same kitchen in front of his family. This charismatic leader of the rubber tappers had been removed.

The word 'sacrifice' comes readily to mind. New worlds are made by Participation, Confrontation, Solidarity and Sacrifice; or maybe a world is made like this out of primaeval chaos for the very first time. But obviously we must be careful. We are not talking about sacrificial suffering for its own sake, as if being killed or wounded will necessarily do anyone any good. Indeed the rubber tappers' association, not to mention the family of Chico Mendes, were greatly harmed and diminished, even embittered, by what happened to him. His death as such was a loss, not a gain. What is creative lies somewhere in whatever it is that leads to a death of this kind. Again we must be careful, since much of what caused it was highly destructive. Chico died because powerful landowners felt threatened, and it is just conceivable that he might have avoided ultimate disaster by going about his campaign in a more productive way. A sacrificial death is not necessarily creative in itself.

W. H. Vanstone once wrote memorably about *Love's Endeavour, Love's Expense.*[6] It is the love which by definition is expensive which is creative. It seeks the good of others, which does not necessarily exclude its own good. It needs to be thoughtful and intelligent: to love with all our mind, or else it will be guided by sentiment and do more harm than good. Through careful reflection on experience and practice it will seek to discern what is best for its neighbours and how to bring that about. But this wholeminded endeavour must be wholehearted as well. It will spare no effort. It will accept the vulnerability that comes from two directions: from those who feel threatened by any alteration to the status quo and can only believe that another's gain is inevitably their loss, and from the exposure that creativity always brings, to which we referred before,[7] where well-intended and carefully thought out initiatives may bring unexpected and negative results. Added to intelligence, vulnerability and courage, love's endeavour is marked by generosity. It is prepared to give what it has to give, including its time, talents, possessions, loyalty and perseverance, in order to achieve its goals. In the extreme it will give all it has to give, as exemplified for me so memorably in the death of Chico Mendes. The mark of creativity then is basically an effective kind of love; but the outcome is inevitably sacrificial. It costs a life if not a death.

Here, then, are what I believe to be four marks of creativity. I have no empirical proof, of course. I can produce a good deal of supporting evidence but none which is beyond dispute. I can only say that I and others have experienced them as creative; and there is a good precedent for not saying much more than that, as we shall presently see.[8] But how do these articles of my creed relate to my Christian faith?

It would be difficult to claim that these ways of being creative or of making a world are peculiarly Christian in character. Some Christians have practised them, Beyers Naude and Chico Mendes among them. But so have many others of other religious faiths and none. They arise out of insights and lessons learned from many different sources, not least in my case from the development movement of the twentieth century and the struggle for human rights. We can, however, ask whether they are compatible or coherent with Christianity, and we shall want to do so if the Christian faith is an important and defining part of our lives. The Bible and tradition are the two most obvious places to look and I shall take two examples: one from tradition, namely the doctrine of atonement, and one from the Bible, namely its witness to Jesus of Nazareth.

If, remembering our Story about making a world with God, we take the idea of 'learning' seriously, as creators with God we are still learning how to make. We have not been told once and for all by some fixed and final revelation and therefore know already all there is to know about how to make. So we shall not necessarily expect to find precisely the same convictions in the Bible and tradition as those we have now arrived at. We may challenge theirs with ours as much as be made to think again by what they have to say. We shall not then look for total agreement but certainly a sense of continuity or family likeness or, as we have said, 'compatibility' or 'coherence' with other ways of looking at the world inspired by the God we know in Christ.

3. Doctrines of atonement

When we look at traditional teaching about the atonement we immediately find a difference of emphasis. The essential image is corrective rather than creative. It understands Christ as primarily the Redeemer who takes away the sins of the world. He puts right what is wrong. He mends what has been broken, including the relationship between God and ourselves. Without denying the need for such a corrective and restorative process, because mistakes are made and human insecurity breeds egotistic behaviour, our own emphasis has been primarily on 'creating' rather than 'redeeming'. We are 'learning how to make', not just 'learning how to mend'. All is not lost, however. Both images have to do with transforming a negative situation into a more positive one, whether it is restoring an originally good creation or creating a world for the first time, turning evil to good or threatening chaos into manageable order.

Teaching about the atonement tries to answer the question: How? How did Christ redeem? What exactly did he do to turn such an unpromising situation around? We can learn from it something of the wonder of our own salvation, but we might also learn how to be part of an ongoing redemptive and creative process. That was confirmed for me when I read F. W. Dillistone's book about atonement many years ago.[9] I have been thankful for it ever since. Dillistone taught me the underlying form of the answer to the question: 'How did Christ redeem?' Answer: 'Well it's rather like this, though it's not exactly like this.' It's rather like, for instance, the wealthy man who buys a slave from his master and then sets him free, though it's not exactly like that. The doctrine deals in analogy.

The work of Christ was unique. It only happened once, and what he accomplished has not been repeated. There is about it something quite strange and fresh and different which we can never entirely understand. But if it were not only strange but totally unlike anything else in our human experience, then we would be unable to understand it at all. It could not be appropriated. It would have no meaning for us and could not be the object of our faith. And clearly there is much about it which is familiar. Indeed the drama of an outstanding human being speaking up for the underdog, challenging authority and being stopped in his tracks by the great and the good, with all the sorrow and heartache it brings in its train, is all too familiar. We have plenty of experience of much the same thing. It happened only once, and yet it happens all the time.

So theories of atonement draw on the familiar in their attempts to shed light on the unfamiliar. They draw on what we do know to help us engage with what we do not know. If Jesus Christ represents God's redemptive or creative action once upon a time it is not unlike the redemptive or creative activity, no doubt energized by the same God, which goes on in human affairs at other times when, for example, slaves are emancipated and debts are cancelled.

This understanding of the nature of Christian doctrine ought to encourage us when we try to set it to work to promote historical change in favour of the poorest. It should make those who regard it as of no practical use think again. It is not all abstract theory. It is not self-contained and sealed up in a world of its own, unable to relate to anything else. It is porous. It is saying that divine redemption and creation work 'rather like this though not exactly like this', and what it is rather like is how redemption and creation work in the everyday world about us. It contains a good deal of wisdom distilled out of a great deal of experience, and if we unpack it it may well be able to teach us and help us. It is certainly worth examining in order to challenge and deepen our own ideas.

There is, of course, no single doctrine of atonement; there are many doctrines. That is why Dillistone referred in his book to 'ranges of comparison'.[10] What happened in the living and dying of Jesus is not to be compared with just one of our more familiar experiences, the emancipation of slaves, for example, but with many, some more recent than others, and where the comparability is persuasive it will not only help in our understanding of the work of Christ but will increase our confidence that such patterns of behaviour are to be emulated, honoured and supported as likely to be redemptive and creative in the here and now.

For me there are strong family likenesses between the four marks of creativity exemplified by the stories I have told and some of the most persistent doctrines of atonement.

1. One of those doctrines, for example, constantly speaks of 'forgiveness'. What Christ has done is rather like that: forgiving

someone, if not exactly like that. Forgiveness belongs very much to the world of redemption and sin where personal responsibility for wrong-doing has to be reckoned with and, as I have said all along, I do not reject that as part of the reality we have to confront. In the background of talk about forgiveness, however, are strong images of exclusion. Sin itself leads to exclusion. The original sin of Adam and Eve put them outside the garden. Sin banishes from the presence of God and isolates us from one another. It breaks relationships. But 'sin' is also a useful label that we use to justify exclusion. It has been applied to the poor more than most. People are justifiably left out, ignored and excluded because they deserve to be left out: lazy, dodgy, irresponsible, inept as they are, and it will generally be better for the insiders if their exclusion is perpetuated. To say that atonement is rather like forgiveness, bringing as it were the sinner back into the fold, is not then entirely at odds with saying that redemption (redeeming the time) or creation (making a world) is rather like Participation. It involves including those who for one bad reason or another have been excluded as being of no account. The old and enduring 'range of comparison' referring to forgiveness is by no means the same, but there is a fruitful sense of continuity and coherence with a more recent one and each has the ability to correct and enlarge the other.

2. What of Confrontation? If there is a classic theory of atonement it is that of Christus Victor. What happened, especially on the cross and at the resurrection, 'is rather like' a battle royal, fought and won, even if it 'is not exactly like' that. The hymns and stories of Easter and Ascension are full of the imagery of Christ's victory over sin and evil and death and the principalities and powers of this world. They are often quite violent and triumphalist images, leaving the enemy totally destroyed. They do not sit easily with more modern talk about non-violence and conflict resolution or, for that matter, with what we know about Jesus himself. We may be tempted to say that what we are involved in is not much like a fight to the death at all. It may be as tough as

that, but it is not so ruthless. There is no easy comparability between Christ as conqueror and the kind of 'confrontation' which we believe can be so creative. They are, however, alike in facing up to evil and chaos rather than accommodating to it, or turning a blind eye and allowing it to continue by default.

3. There is, perhaps, a more sympathetic relationship between Solidarity as a mark of creativity and those traditional doctrines of atonement, or explanations of how God in Christ redeems and recreates, which focus more on the incarnation than the cross. To quote the familiar words of Irenaeus: 'Jesus Christ . . . was made what we are, that he might make us completely what He is'.[11] He became like us that we might become like him. There are, of course, many strands to that traditional teaching. In becoming man God grows in understanding of our lot. Christ recapitulates or goes over again all our tragic human history, undoing the evil we have done step by step. And when he comes, this God in man, he 'infects' us with the potency of his divine life. There are no simple parallels to all of that, though there are resonances with what we know happens when people stand by each other. The overwhelming image, however, is of someone who for understandable reasons is perceived as being on the other side: he is God not man, holy not sinful, wealthy and powerful not poor, but is now discovered to be firmly on our side. Images of incarnation and Solidarity meet in Emmanuel: God with us, and in Kenosis or self-emptying, where this Christ does not cling on to the best of both worlds. He does not cling to equality with God. He does not stay safely on one side whilst sympathizing with the other. The one is given up to be radically identified with the other.

4. The understanding of Christ's death as a sacrifice has been closely associated with the idea that atonement has been brought about and forgiveness made possible because the price has been paid. We have only to repent and have faith. The perfect sacrificial victim has been found. The ransom money has been handed over. It's 'rather like' those ancient views of sacrifice

where a life is required for a life, or the way debtors and slaves are bought out of their troubles, even though it is 'not exactly like' that. Such views carry within them uncomfortable echoes of some Shylock demanding his pound of flesh, even if the one who demands it is in this case identical to the one who gives. The quality of mercy, according to sacrificial theories, does appear to be constrained in this way. There is no such thing as free forgiveness. Heinous crimes have been committed against God. They must be taken seriously. The law must be upheld. There is a penalty for sin. Someone must be punished, if not everyone. Much of the emphasis appears to fall on the cost of sin whereas, according to our understanding of the Sacrifice which is creative, it ought to fall on the cost of love. These ranges of comparison, ancient and modern, all referring to sacrifice have points to make to each other. The one may misunderstand the nature of evil and its consequences. The other may underestimate them. Nevertheless they agree that neither a better world nor a new world can be had on the cheap. The route is by way of a cross, not round it: one of the many lessons about creativity we find so difficult to learn.

4. Jesus of Nazareth

I suggested there were two places to look when we ask whether our own convictions, in this case about creativity or how to make a world, are compatible or coherent with Christianity. The second is the Bible and perhaps above all its witness to Jesus of Nazareth. If he is the ultimate measure of our faith, can our convictions survive in his light and shadow? If his story is the ultimate paradigm, are my paradigmatic stories at ease with his?

There seems to me to be no great difficulty in characterizing the life and ministry of Jesus as marked by Participation, Confrontation, Solidarity and Sacrifice.

1. Some will claim that the central message of Jesus was about the forgiveness of sins, but in the society of his day the close

relationship between a sinner and being an outcast was not hard to see. The lines of demarcation between insiders and outsiders were said to be about morality, but were not really about morality at all since there was little to choose between those on either side. The lines were really about prejudice and power and, although forgiveness is always needed whichever side of the line we are on, when Jesus forgave it often had more to do with bringing the excluded in from the cold. Being forgiven came close to being included. Those who were regarded as unclean or offenders and on the wrong side of the law were now apparently welcome to be part of the enterprise. Prodigals came home. Those who were normally left off the guest list were now invited. There are even indications that life might be enriched by embracing the opposition. The suspect Samaritan after all turned out to be a real asset to the man, presumably a Jew, who fell among thieves; and the injunction to love your enemies may be more interesting than just one more moral demand on us. Perhaps it is not an 'ought' but an 'is'. It could be an astute piece of advice suggesting that, as a matter of fact, far more resources will be available to us if we work with people we tend to regard as the opposition than if we keep them safely at arms length or work against them. Jesus goes about things in a highly participative way.

2. He is also confrontational. He belongs to the Magnificat people. He causes dissension between relatives. He is openly critical of prominent figures. He speaks out against what he regards as the misuse of the law: the Sabbath law, for example. It was designed to be humane but it had been turned into a burden, often a crushing one, where rules and regulations took precedence over human need. Perhaps the most striking confrontational image is of Jesus deliberately deciding to go to Jerusalem and ride into a storm which he could just as easily have walked away from. Once there he refuses to keep quiet but denounces the misuse of the Temple, where the poor and the outsider were so badly treated, and dares to announce where he believes a more peaceful future for the city will be found, so putting himself on a

collision course with the religious and imperial authorities. He said himself that he brought not peace but a sword, even if he told the disciples to put their particular kind of sword away.

3. The baptism of Jesus by John is a good example of solidarity. It was described as a baptism for the forgiveness of sins. Whatever his own awareness of sin may have been, this Messiah, anointed by God and carrying all the expectations of his people, declares that he is unequivocally on their side. He is one of them, even when it comes to acts of repentance for wrongdoing he has come to redeem rather than commit or perpetuate. He remains throughout his ministry the friend of outcasts, tax collectors and sinners, the deranged and untouchable. He is not uncritical of an adulterous woman, or a convicted thief, or an unruly mob, but they know whose side he is on. His 'aloneness' at the end, outside the walls of the city and seemingly abandoned by God, is a final, striking but ironic picture of where his loyalties lay.

4. Looking at the life and work of Jesus, it goes almost without saying that this attempt to love with all his mind and heart and soul was not without cost. He warned others that it would be the same for them as they set out to build their towers and fight their battles. His death had no particular merit in itself, though some like Judas may have thought that by provoking it they could usefully bring matters to a head. It was not required as such. It was his ministry that was required: to the weak and the powerful, to the insider and the outsider, to the righteous and the sinner. A sacrificial death was not the point of it all but it was the consequence. Beverley Harrison expresses it perfectly:

Orthodox, Christological interpretations imply that somehow the entire meaning of Jesus' life and work is to be found in his headlong race toward Golgotha, towards crucifixion – as if he sought suffering as an end in itself to complete the resolution of the divine human drama once and for all. I believe that this way of viewing Jesus' work robs it of its – and his – moral radicality. Jesus was radical not in his lust for sacrifice but in his power of mutuality. Jesus' death on a cross, his sacrifice, was no abstract exercise in moral virtue. His death was the price he paid for refusing to abandon the radical activity of love – of expressing solidarity and reciprocity with the excluded ones in his community.[12]

There is no great difficulty, then, in getting the biblical witness to Jesus to confirm me in my belief that creativity is marked by Participation, Confrontation, Solidarity and Sacrifice. But it is notoriously easy, as we all know, to go round in circles. We claim Jesus as the inspirer and measurer of our faith, but we appeal to accounts of him which we have already made to mirror the image of what we believe. The biblical story which is meant to confirm our convictions as Christ-like has already been coloured by those same convictions. We read out of the biblical material what we have previously read into it. Christians have always done it. The biblical writers do it themselves; now we do it, so that quoting the Gospels in evidence is another way of stating our beliefs rather than a way of testing them out against independent criteria. In my case I am simply reading 'The Developers' Bible' that I have previously written.

We cannot escape entirely from this dilemma. We can make sure we read the whole of the biblical witness and not just those parts of it which suit our preconceptions. There are, for example, some pretty difficult sayings in the Gospels (let alone the rest of the Bible!) where Jesus condemns and dismisses his enemies which don't fit easily with all our talk of solidarity and inclusion. Probably the most effective guard against over-subjective accounts of Jesus, however, is to live in the wider Christian community where everybody else's views are as incomplete and unsatisfactory and coloured to suit themselves as are our own, but fortunately tend to be incomplete and unsatisfactory in different ways. By coming up against them we become aware of the differences between us, rich and poor, for example, and there is some hope of our own faith being challenged and made more complete by theirs, and theirs perhaps by ours. That is what we do when we test our faith against the long tradition of the church and what Christians have believed in the past, about atonement, for example. We are living in the wider Christian community. That is what we are also doing when we try to learn more about what other Christians think and believe today, especially for us the Christians of the East and of the South rather than of the North and of the West.

Even if, after all that, these characteristics of the ministry of Jesus stand up, there is no sure proof that they are creative and some of the best ways to go about making a world. Many factors contributed to the outcome of his work and it is difficult to trace the lines of cause and effect and demonstrate how much, if anything, was owed, for example, to the solidarity of Jesus with the outcasts of his day. Even if we could trace those lines, the immediate result is hardly reassuring and the long-term result, as we argued when we discussed the impact of Christianity, is even less so. Jesus was killed. His followers were persecuted. Jerusalem was destroyed. The Jews experienced war and exile rather than peace. The church chose a similar war-like path once it got hold of the reins of power. The world still looks decidedly unlike the Kingdom which was about to arrive two thousand years ago. It all looks more like impotence than creativity!

What we do know, however, is that all that had happened came to be experienced by the early Christians (Luke 24 and the story of the journey to Emmaus registers initial disappointment) as highly creative. It seemed to them that a whole new way of life in a new community with new relationships where there were no more strangers but a single household was now a real possibility. They even spoke about a new creation. A world had been made![13] This is the not the place to discuss the resurrection at any length, but for me that sense of creativity is the essence of the resurrection experience. It is not that Christ has been vindicated and the shame and ignominy of the cross has been reversed, not least because the cross, or rather the love it epitomized, was far from a shame. It is not that we now have proof positive that the old enemy, death, has been overcome and there is life beyond the grave. We don't. It is not that the final act has been played out in the drama of redemption. Our experience denies it. Its importance does not depend on successfully arguing that the body of Jesus got up and walked away. We can't. None of these ideas is without its wisdom, but the essence of the resurrection experience is that, unpromising in many ways as it all seemed, the costly living and dying of Jesus of Nazareth had within them and had released within our human life, like some positive viral infection, a fresh and creative dynamism, so that to reflect on how he lived and died is to learn crucial lessons about how to make a world and how a world is being made in which men and women can flourish and be at home.

5. Conclusion

I have described what I have come to regard as four marks of creativity, or lessons I have learned about how to make a world. They are not peculiarly Christian and they are all the better for that, but they are compatible and coherent with the Bible and Christian tradition. If we want to be constructive in the struggle against poverty and injustice they strongly suggest a number of ways to go about it. They are not the only ways. They have been learned in the school of development. There are other schools to go to, conflict resolution, for example. For that and other reasons there are other lessons to learn. These are not the only marks of creativity,[14] and they are not, of course, to be treated in isolation. They have an organic interrelationship with each other as my paradigmatic stories about Beyers Naude or Chico Mendes demonstrate. Participation and Solidarity are close allies, crossing boundaries as they both do, and taken together with Confronting the fearful measures we take against others in the hope of protecting ourselves they go a long way to making love the costly and Sacrificial business that it is. These marks cannot easily be separated from one another, nor can they be divorced from the other issues we need to reflect on in the pastoral cycle when we try to discern the next steps we should take. There are at least three, as we have seen,[15] and not just one; analysis and goals as well as process. We must not only learn how to get things done. We must not only discuss ways and means or 'process'. We need to analyse the situations we are dealing with if we are to avoid making completely false moves, like dealing with perversity when we should be dealing with insecurity. And we need to set our goals in line with all we know of God's will for us and the shape of God's Kingdom. These four marks of creativity need that context otherwise, combined, they could become a very powerful force for entirely the wrong purposes.

For example, I remember encountering a highly influential Hindu woman in South India. She was in her sixties and had worked all her life with landless women in the state of Tamil Nadu. She was a qualified lawyer who could have enjoyed a successful and professional career. Instead she helped the dispossessed to win land and provide for themselves and their children. Her methods were highly participative. She did not act on behalf of these women as if they could do nothing for themselves. She mobilized them and acted with them. Their approach was very confrontational indeed, either beleaguering government officials, or bearding the landowners in their dens, or pursuing matters in the courts, or occupying temples, or marching and demonstrating noisily round the perimeters of land which they claimed was theirs. The matter was never allowed to rest. Her solidarity with these women was obvious. On every reckoning her natural place was on the other side to them, with the educated and wealthy élite, not with the Dalits. But she was clearly on their side, and not without cost. She had sacrificed a lucrative career. She had suffered at the hands of powerful landowners. She and her husband had no property, only a prayer mat, a few clothes, a lamp for worship, some books and a spinning wheel. They slept where they were invited in. This woman, so Christlike in many ways, was a Hindu, proving yet again that creativity is no Christian prerogative; but she was no saint, and it was not difficult to imagine her great strength being used in the wrong cause. History is full of examples. 'Learning how to make' will be of little creative use if we do not also learn how to analyse, in her case why so many were landless, and set Christlike goals for our endeavours.

Once they have been named, these marks of creativity may seem almost obvious and non-controversial, but it is sobering to compare them with some of our assumptions about what still passes for redemptive and creative activity. How difficult it is to discern them, for example, in the inexpensive, undisruptive evangelistic programmes of our churches. The example I know best is the 'charity business'. It is easy to deal in caricatures and indeed to misrepresent large numbers of devoted people who give massive amounts of time and energy and show inordinate degrees of kindness in charitable causes. But take the now familiar image of the soup-run on a cold night which was made controversial just before Christmas 1999 by the government-appointed 'Tsar for the Homeless'. She criticized it for its false analysis of the problem and for its mistaken goals, but on any reckoning it is distinctly devoid of anything resembling participation or solidarity or confrontation or sacrifice. It is a kindness done to those on the other side of a social and economic divide without confronting the underlying issues, and it is done at some inconvenience but no great cost. Similar worries arise when it comes to Northern agencies working in international development, some carrying overtly Christian labels. Many have taken seriously the need, for example, for the poorest of the poor to participate in their own development. But the involvement of the relatively rich in this great enterprise is more problematic. There is a great deal of genuine concern and commitment. There are, perhaps, hopeful signs of growing solidarity in terms of mutual support between people all round the world as they campaign together on issues like debt cancellation and fair trade. But much of it can still look uncomfortably like what Charles Elliott once called 'Comfortable Compassion'[16] offered at a safe distance. Much else could well be beyond the majority of us, but whilst our response to poverty and injustice seems so far from taking seriously on board the lessons we are supposedly learning about how new worlds are made, we shall not be too surprised that all-too-much of the world and its poverty remains stubbornly the same.

5

CHOOSING TO HOPE

In these four reflections at the interface between poverty and Christianity I began with two experienced challenges to my Christian faith: the challenge of suffering as 'normal' and the challenge of the apparent ineffectiveness of the Christian enterprise which claims to redeem the times. What emerged was a personal bias in favour of theological work which promotes historical change in favour of the poor, remembering that much of that work can be indifferent, even hostile towards them. I have touched on three examples.

The first is storytelling, where the 'Story' (or, if you like, the narrative form of systematic theology) does not explain the status quo in order to justify it, but to support and encourage those who seek to change it for something better by making some sense of what they do. For me it is a Story about a God who is busy making a world out of chaos for the very first time and who draws us into these costly endeavours. I personally find it supportive, not least because it reminds me that we are not left to generate the creative energies required all on our own. They are a given, seen and experienced in the active loving kindness which is everywhere within our relationships, buoying us up and offering us far more than it ever demands. But supportive as the Story is, I am aware, sometimes acutely aware, of the difficulties in telling it: moral, emotional and intellectual, especially in a 'post-Modern' world where one man's Story is another man's fantasy.

My second example of theological work promoting historical change had to do with methodology or ways of doing social ethics, social theology, practical theology and theological reflection on practice. Though often regarded as afterthoughts or the poor relations of theology, these are, in fact, the crown of our theological endeavours. But when it comes to social policy-making and, for me especially, development policy-making, how do you draw on your Christian faith to inform your answers to those three recurring questions about analysis, goals, and the ways and means or process of achieving them? Some remain sceptical that Christianity as such will have much to contribute. I well understand that scepticism, which an abstract and indifferent Western theology has often brought on itself, but I don't entirely share it.

The third example of theological work promoting change was to take the third question, about process, and draw attention to four ways of being creative or of moving from where we are towards where we want to be, which have been learned by those involved in development and the struggle against poverty and which are compatible or coherent with Christian tradition and the biblical witness to Jesus. We should not expect to achieve our goals unless we take them seriously. Along with the need to achieve a better balance of power, they illustrate how rules of thumb can be useable tests for shaping our Christian obedience.

As I hinted at in my Introduction, there is an underlying text or agenda in all of this which I have not discussed explicitly. Christian belief for me, as for many, is quite difficult (even if unbelief is not necessarily distressing) partly because of experiences of poverty and injustice and partly because of the pluralist and relativist culture of 'post-Modernism'. Whether we are talking about our Stories or our practical commitments, how are our beliefs to be validated?[1] Implicit in what I have said are some answers. They include a concern for coherence between, for example, the insights we cull from current experience and the more subtle but not infallible teaching of the church; and consensus building between various interested parties committed to the same cause. They recognize the importance of dialogue and interdisciplinary testing, but above all they link the validity of what we believe to its fruitfulness in promoting change in favour of the poorest. There is an ongoing debate about whether theology is validated by 'praxis' and whether truth lies in liberating actions or right teaching where, incidentally, liberation theologians are not always on the side you would expect.[2] I am in no position to resolve it, but if praxis is not the whole of the answer it is for me a very big part of it. Does our theological work, systematic and practical, contribute at the end of the day to good news for the poor?

The three examples I have touched on do not exhaust the kinds of theological work I am attracted to. Let me mention two more. First, although we have said something about 'analysis' and 'process', we have said little or nothing about clarifying the values which are rooted in Christian belief and which shape our goals or our vision of the world we aspire to create with God. Embodying them in our life together is, I think, largely the theological work we find, for example, in discussions about Christian Socialism.[3] Second, we have not discussed liturgy as a regular and powerful instrument of Christian formation. It is in the liturgy that the Story of God's costly creativity gets into our system. It is probably the most important way in which Christian faith influences our Christian action: by forming us into men and women who think and feel and decide and behave in a certain kind of way. But that leaves a good many important questions to sort out. If, for example, liturgy is primarily the worship of God, allowing the transcendent to distract us from the mundane, how does it maintain that primary focus on God and in so doing nourish our commitment to the poor rather than breed indifference? Or again, if liturgy rehearses the primary Story of God's actions in Christ, to what extent should it be neutral rather than biased in relation to the many Christianities of the rich and the poor which those actions have inspired?

So there is a good deal more to be said about the various aspects of 'pastoral cycling' or the interaction of faith and practice,

Christianity and poverty. I hope that what has been said will not sound like a bald speech in favour of so-called 'practical theology' and against 'systematic theology', since I have been careful to indicate the contributions which systematic theology can make to the construction of God's Kingdom. What I have said might, however, sound like a piece of crude advice to keep our heads down and get on with the practical tasks to hand when the outlook in general looks unpromising. If there is not much faith and hope around, at least there can be moral obedience. If the 'poetry' won't flow, let's get on with the 'prose'. I confess that that is very often all I am left with when my Story or theological system crashes; but whilst I think it is a fair reflection of the persistent sense of moral claim that remains with me when all else fails, it misrepresents my understanding of Christian hope.

Let me conclude with one more experience. On a visit to the Horn of Africa I met a pastor from the Mekanu Jesu Evangelical church. I stood with him in one of the most unpromising landscapes I have ever seen. Seventy or eighty years ago the hills surrounding his village were covered in trees. Today they were all gone and with them the gentle rains and the soil and the crops. Literally, there were no grounds for hope as far as anyone could see. The pastor, who might have been expected to concentrate on preaching a gospel of the forgiveness of sins rather than trying to create a new heaven on earth for the poor, took me to his tree-nursery where fifty to a hundred saplings were growing. He told me he intended to plant those trees and the others he would propagate all over the distant hills and back again until the land became green and fertile.

This reminded me of my Story of a God who looked out on to an empty void, chaotic, without shape or form, and of how unpromising the sight must have been; and of how God in Christ, 'late in time', looked out on the even greater disorder and misery that men and women had made out of their fears and insecurity, and how doubly unpromising that sight must have been. There was little hope to be had out of either of them. Hope, however, may be a choice we make and not a conclusion we draw. It may be something bred into such unpromising scenarios rather than bled out of them. The Evangelical pastor chose to hope in the barren hills that surrounded his people. He chose to believe they had a future; just as God chose to hope and believe that a formless void and a loveless world had a future; just as we choose to believe in the future of some unpromising personality or scenario well known to us. That choice to have faith in someone's potential can make all the difference in the world, generating confidence and opening up possibilities which otherwise would never have existed. That choice can fill the otherwise unpromising with a good deal of promise. Hope is not abandoned in favour of obedience. Obedience becomes the midwife of hope.

The pastor's story and God's story make several things clearer for me. First, hope is not a guarantee that all shall be well. That is a guarantee we cannot have. The most that faith can offer is the confidence that grows from our encounters, above all in Christ, with an unbroken spirit and a persistent love that will do all it can to ensure that all manner of thing shall be well whether it succeeds or not. Second, hope as we know is not optimism, breezily expecting the best for no obvious good reason. Third, although we shall have perfectly understandable mood swings, Christian hope is not something given to us by circumstances that cheer us up. It is not reactive, here today when things are going well and gone tomorrow when things are going badly. Hope, rather, is proactive. It is something we choose to have by believing in the people and places we love, however unpromising they may seem, and by treating them as if they had a promising future.

By choosing to believe that the world has possibilities, possibilities arise where otherwise they would not have done. That is true of God and it is true of us. By regarding the world we know, marked by the chaos of insecurity and the normality and persistence of poverty and injustice, as promising and acting accordingly, it is filled with promise. We do not reap hope as a reward. We do not receive it only as a gift. Hope is not reactive. Hope is creative. It is not the child of transformation. Transformation is the child of hope. It makes the hills green and it believes that all things can be made new.

NOTES

Introduction

1. See, for example, Gerald Prunier, *The Rwanda Crisis*, Hurst 1995.
2. See also Michael Taylor, *Good for the Poor: Christian Ethics and World Development*, Mowbray 1990.

1. The Normality of Suffering

1. I am helpfully reminded, by Alan Suggate in conversation and by correspondence, that philosophers caution against being over-impressed by the 'quantity' of suffering since it does not affect its moral acceptability. The effect of its seeming 'normality' on me, however, remains.
2. *The Brothers Karamazov*, part II, book v, chapter iv.
3. See, for example, Barry Whitney, *Theodicy: An Annotated Bibliography on the Problem of Evil, 1960–1990*, Bowlingreen, Ohio 1998.
4. John Hick, *Evil and the God of Love*, Collins Fontana 1968, p. 399.
5. Ibid., pp. 366f.
6. Ibid., p. 380.
7. In, for example, *Death and Eternal Life*, Collins 1976.
8. Frances Young, *Face to Face*, Epworth Press 1985; second edition T&T Clark 1990.
9. See, for example, Frances Young, *Can These Dry Bones Live?*, SCM Press 1982, p. 58.
10. Ibid., pp. 57f. Young is quoting Simone Weil, *On Science, Necessity and the Love of God*, OUP 1968.
11. Ibid., pp. 58f., 78; and *Face to Face*, p. 163.
12. *Can These Dry Bones Live?*, pp. 80f.; and *Face to Face*, p. 92.
13. *Face to Face*, p. 185.
14. W. H. Vanstone, *Love's Endeavour, Love's Expense*, Darton, Longman & Todd 1977.

15. Ibid., p. 47.
16. Ibid., p. 48.
17. John Parratt, *Reinventing Christianity*, Eerdmans 1995.
18. Catholic Institute for International Relations and British Council of Churches 1985.
19. In Parratt, *Reinventing Christianity*, p. 170.
20. Aloysius Pieris, *An Asian Theology of Liberation*, T&T Clark 1988, p. 88.
21. Ibid.
22. Eleazar Fernandez, *Toward a Theology of Struggle*, Orbis, Maryknoll 1994.
23. Ibid., p. 36.
24. Ibid., p. 39.
25. Andrew Sung Park, *The Wounded Heart of God*, Abingdon, Nashville 1993, p. 10.
26. Ibid., pp. 77–81.
27. See ibid., p. 133, where Park argues against the unhealthy separation of orthodoxy and orthopraxis, usually by neglecting the latter.
28. Ibid., pp. 72f.
29. Ibid., p. 8.
30. Gustavo Gutiérrez, *On Job: God-talk and the Suffering of the Innocent*, Orbis, Maryknoll 1986.
31. Ibid., pp. xvf.
32. Ibid., p. 102; 'Ayacucho' is a Quechuan word meaning 'the corner of the dead'.
33. Ibid., p. 82.
34. Ibid., p. 86.
35. See, for example, the apologetic (not apologizing) tone of the Preface to John Hick's *Evil and the God of Love*, where his attempt to respond to the challenge of evil to the Christian faith is said to be 'addressed both to Christian believers and to the agnostics, sceptics, and humanists who are the more characteristic citizens of the intellectual world of today', p. x.

2. The Impact of Christianity

1. *North–South: A Programme for Survival*, Pan Books 1980.
2. See p. 29 above.
3. Eleazar Fernandez, *Toward a Theology of Struggle*, Orbis, Maryknoll 1994, p. 36.
4. Compare the brief overviews of Christian teaching in Andrew Sung

Park, *The Wounded Heart of God*, Abingdon, Nashville 1993, pp. 10f. and 70–72. Reinhold Niebuhr wrote about sin and insecurity in *The Nature and Destiny of Man*, Parts I and II, Scribners, New York 1949; see Part I, pp. 178ff. He describes man's insecurity as the 'occasion' though not the 'cause' of sin.

5. See pp. 19f. above.
6. Walter Wink, *The Powers that Be*, Doubleday, New York 1998 is to some extent a digest of his trilogy of books on the Powers and of *Violence and Nonviolence in South Africa*, New Society, Philadelphia 1987.
7. Walter Wink, *Engaging the Powers*, Fortress Press, Minneapolis 1992, p. 69.
8. A theme running through Alan Wilkinson, *Christian Socialism: Scott Holland to Tony Blair*, SCM Press 1998.
9. Don Cupitt has linked the Kingdom with post-Modernity; see *Kingdom Come in Everyday Speech*, SCM Press 2000.
10. See her remarks in *Face to Face*, second edition T&T Clark 1990, pp. 141, 189, 206f.
11. See pp. 15ff. above.
12. See p. 17 above.
13. Rosino Gibellini (ed.), *Frontiers of Theology in Latin America*, SCM Press 1980, contains useful chapters by a range of authors even if the 'frontiers' may have moved since they wrote.
14. In ibid., p. 145.
15. In ibid., pp. 264f.
16. See p. 27 above.
17. In *Frontiers of Theology in Latin America*, p. 149.
18. In ibid., p. 28.
19. In ibid., p. 288.
20. In ibid., pp. 28f.

3. Christian Doctrine and Development Policy

1. Co-operating with CAFOD (England and Wales), SCIAF (Scotland) and TROICARE (Ireland), the Roman Catholic agencies.
2. See pp. 61f. above.
3. See p. 3 above.
4. In chapter 4 below.
5. See Michael Taylor, *Not Angels but Agencies*, SCM Press and WCC 1999, pp. 101–4.
6. For example, in Ronald H. Preston, *Confusions in Christian Social*

Ethics, SCM Press 1994 and *The Future of Ecumenical Social Thought*, report of an informal discussion in Berlin, 1992. Both tend to be critical of the WCC's approach in more recent years.

7. In, for example, *Against the Stream*, SCM Press 1954.
8. Penguin 1942, re-issued SPCK 1976.
9. See *Not Angels but Agencies*, pp. 65f.
10. See Michael Taylor, *Past Their Sell-By Date? NGOs and Their Future in Development*, the Seventh Bradford Development Lecture, University of Bradford 1997.
11. See *Not Angels but Agencies*, p. 168.
12. See chapter 2, p. 45 above.
13. See pp. 108–13 below.
14. Michael Northcott, *Life After Debt*, SPCK 1999, pp. 171–81.
15. Oliver O'Donovan, *The Desire of Nations: Re-discovering the Roots of Political Theology*, CUP 1996.
16. Michael Northcott, *Life After Debt*, ibid.

4. Learning How to Make

1. See, for example, Reinhold Niebuhr, *Moral Man and Immoral Society*, Scribners, New York 1960.
2. See Michael Northcott's discussion of participation as a value crucial to social transformation in *Life After Debt*, SPCK 1999, p. 145.
3. Catholic Institute for International Relations and British Council of Churches 1985.
4. See, for example, Jacques Ellul, *Violence*, SCM Press 1970.
5. Walter Wink, *The Powers That Be*, Doubleday, New York 1998.
6. Darton Longman & Todd 1977.
7. See p. 22 above.
8. See p. 117 below.
9. F. W. Dillistone, *The Christian Understanding of Atonement*, Nisbet 1968.
10. Ibid., p. 23.
11. In ibid., p. 52.
12. 'The Power of Anger in the Work of Love' in *Making the Connections: Essays in Feminist Social Ethics*, Beacon Press, Boston 1985; included in Ann Loades (ed.), *Feminist Theology: A Reader*, SPCK 1990, p. 210.
13. See, for example, Eph. 2; II Cor. 5; Rev. 21.
14. Others may be 'Non-violence' as discussed by Walter Wink in *The*

Powers That Be; 'Compassionate Connectedness' as discussed by
Andrew Sung Park in the *Wounded Heart of God*, Abingdon,
Nashville 1993, p. 108; and 'Gift-giving' as discussed by Michael
Northcott in *Life After Debt*, p. 68.

15. See p. 87f. above.
16. Charles Elliott, *Comfortable Compassion*, Hodder 1987.

5. Choosing to Hope

1. David Kamitsuka's discussion of this question in *Theology and
Contemporary Culture*, CUP 1999, is demanding but helpful.
2. See, for example, Kamitsuka's many references to Clodovis Boss in
ibid.
3. See Alan Wilkinson, *Christian Socialism: Scott Holland to Tony
Blair*, SCM Press 1998.

INDEX

India, 38, 40, 75, 119
International Financial Institutions, 49, 67, 97
Insecurity, 22, 47–9, 63, 88, 95, 108, 119, 125–6, 130
Irenaeus, 112

Job, 19–20, 31–3, 129
Jubilee 2000, 41
Justice, 89

Kairos Document, 27, 60, 102
Kamitsuka, David, 132
Kingdom of God, 15, 43–4, 53, 55–8, 62–3, 89, 97, 117, 119, 125, 130

Liberation, 27–8, 31, 36, 65–6, 71, 96, 102
Liberation theology, 28, 31, 66, 76, 86, 124, 129
Liturgy, 124
Love, 14–15, 17–22, 24–5, 32–4, 43, 47–8, 50, 53–4, 57, 63, 65–6, 89, 95, 107, 113–18, 126

Marx, Karl, 28, 36
Middle-axioms, 73
Minjung, 29
Mendes, Chico, 105–7, 118

Naude, Beyers, 103–4, 107, 118
Niebuhr, Reinhold, 95–6, 130–1
Northcott, Michael, 89–90, 131–2

Orthopraxis, 31, 129

Park, Andrew Sung, 29–31, 129–30, 132
Parratt, John, 26–7, 129
Pastoral cycle, 5, 41, 86, 119

Participation, 29, 74–9, 82–5, 87, 94, 99, 100, 106, 111, 113, 116, 118, 120, 131
Perversity, 3–4, 16, 30, 45–9, 63, 88, 95, 119
Pieris, Aloysius, 28, 129
Pluralism, 79, 83
Post-Modernity, 64, 130
Power, 20–1, 24, 50, 59, 61, 66, 90, 95–7, 114, 116–17, 123, 131
Preston, R.H., 130
Principalities and Powers, 43, 48, 111
Progress, 29, 52, 54, 59, 62, 64, 83, 88, 106

Reconciliation, 3–3, 27, 43, 45, 56, 70, 87, 102
Refugees, 1–2, 31, 40, 70, 106
Relativism, 29, 83–4
Repentance, 3–4, 45–6, 50, 87, 115
Resurrection, 111, 117–8
Romero, Archbishop, 102
Rwanda, 1–4, 41, 44–7, 70, 87, 128

Sacrifice, 18, 61, 106, 112–13, 116, 119–20
Senegal, 103–4
Sin, 4, 18–19, 30–1, 33–4, 44–6, 48, 55–6, 59, 61, 63, 111, 113, 115, 130
Social ethics, 68–9, 72, 76, 78, 83–4, 86, 122, 130–1
Solidarity, 3, 66, 103–6, 112–13, 115–20
Somalia, 97–9
Stories, 41, 49, 63–7, 83, 97, 110–11, 113, 118, 123
Suggate, Alan, 128
Systematic theology, 66, 122, 125

Temple, William, 73